Cram101 Textbook Outlines to accompany:

The Elements of Statistical Learning

Hastie, 2nd Edition

A Content Technologies Inc. publication (c) 2011.

STUDYING MADE EASY

This Craml0l notebook is designed to make studying easier and increase your comprehension of the textbook material. Instead of starting with a blank notebook and trying to write down everything discussed in class lectures, you can use this Craml0l textbook notebook and annotate your notes along with the lecture.

Our goal is to give you the best tools for success.

For a supreme understanding of the course, pair your notebook with our online tools. Should you decide you prefer Craml0l.com as your study tool,

we'd like to offer you a trade...

Our Trade In program is a simple way for us to keep our promise and provide you the best studying tools, regardless of where you purchased your Craml0l textbook notebook. As long as your notebook is in *Like New Condition**, you can send it back to us and we will immediately give you a Craml0l.com account free for 120 days!

Let The *Trade In* Begin!

THREE SIMPLE STEPS TO TRADE:

1. Go to www.cram101.com/tradein and fill out the packing slip information.

2. Submit and print the packing slip and mail it in with your Craml0l textbook notebook.

3. Activate your account after you receive your email confirmation.

* Books must be returned in *Like New Condition*, meaning there is no damage to the book including, but not limited to; ripped or torn pages, markings or writing on pages, or folded / creased pages. Upon receiving the book, Craml0l will inspect it and reserves the right to terminate your free Craml0l.com account and return your textbook notebook at the owners expense.

Learning System

Cram101 Textbook Outlines is a learning system. The notes in this book are the highlights of your textbook, you will never have to highlight a book again.

How to use this book. Take this book to class, it is your notebook for the lecture. The notes and highlights on the left hand side of the pages follow the outline and order of the textbook. All you have to do is follow along while your instructor presents the lecture. Circle the items emphasized in class and add other important information on the right side. With Cram101 Textbook Outlines you'll spend less time writing and more time listening. Learning becomes more efficient.

Cram101.com Online

Increase your studying efficiency by using Cram101.com's practice tests and online reference material. It is the perfect complement to Cram101 Textbook Outlines. Use self-teaching matching tests or simulate in-class testing with comprehensive multiple choice tests, or simply use Cram's true and false tests for quick review. Cram101.com even allows you to enter your in-class notes for an integrated studying format combining the textbook notes with your class notes.

Visit **www.Cram101.com**, click Sign Up at the top of the screen, and enter **DK73DW13705** in the promo code box on the registration screen. Your access to www.Cram101.com is discounted by 50% because you have purchased this book. Sign up and stop highlighting textbooks forever.

The Elements of Statistical Learning
Hastie, 2nd

CONTENTS

1. Overview of Supervised Learning 2
2. Linear Methods for Regression 18
3. Linear Methods for Classification 28
4. Basis Expansions and Regularization 42
5. Kernel Smoothing Methods 58
6. Model Assessment and Selection 64
7. Model Inference and Averaging 74
8. Additive Models, Trees, and Related Methods 86
9. Boosting and Additive Trees 98
10. Neural Networks 100
11. Support Vector Machines and Flexible Discriminants/Prototype Methods 106
12. Unsupervised Learning 116
13. Random Forests/Ensemble Learning 126
14. Undirected Graphical Models 130
15. High-Dimensional Problems 136

Chapter 1. Overview of Supervised Learning

Independent variable	The terms `dependent variable` and `Independent variable` are used in similar but subtly different ways in mathematics and statistics as part of the standard terminology in those subjects. They are used to distinguish between two types of quantities being considered, separating them into those available at the start of a process and those being created by it, where the latter (dependent variables) are dependent on the former (Independent variables). The Independent variable is typically the variable being manipulated or changed and the dependent variable is the observed result of the Independent variable being manipulated.
Discrete probability distributions	Discrete probability distributions arise in the mathematical description of probabilistic and statistical problems in which the values that might be observed are restricted to being within a pre-defined list of possible values. This list has either a finite number of members, or at most is countable. In probability theory, a probability distribution is called discrete if it is characterized by a probability mass function. Thus, the distribution of a random variable X is discrete, and X is then called a discrete random variable, if $$\sum_{u} \Pr(X = u) = 1$$ as u runs through the set of all possible values of X.
Dummy variable	In regression analysis, a Dummy variable is one that takes the values 0 or 1 to indicate the absence or presence of some categorical effect that may be expected to shift the outcome. For example, in econometric time series analysis, Dummy variables may be used to indicate the occurrence of wars, or major strikes. It could thus be thought of as a truth value represented as a numerical value 0 or 1.
Least squares	The method of Least squares is a standard approach to the approximate solution of overdetermined systems, i.e. sets of equations in which there are more equations than unknowns. `Least squares` means that the overall solution minimizes the sum of the squares of the errors made in solving every single equation. The most important application is in data fitting. The best fit in the Least squares sense minimizes the sum of squared residuals, a residual being the difference between an observed value and the fitted value provided by a model.

Chapter 1. Overview of Supervised Learning

Linear model	In statistics, the term Linear model is used in different ways according to the context. The most common occurrence is in connection with regression models and the term is often taken as synonymous with linear regression model. However the term is also used in time series analysis with a different meaning.

Here the statistical model is as follows. Given a (random) sample $(Y_i, X_{i1}, \ldots, X_{ip}), \ i = 1, \ldots, n$ the relation between the observations Y_i and the independent variables X_{ij} is formulated as

$$Y_i = \beta_0 + \beta_1 \phi_1(X_{i1}) + \cdots + \beta_p \phi_p(X_{ip}) + \varepsilon_i \qquad i = 1, \ldots, n$$

where $\phi_1, \ldots, \phi_p$ may be nonlinear functions. In the above, the quantities ε_i are random variables representing errors in the relationship. The `linear` part of the designation relates to the appearance of the regression coefficients, β_j in a linear way in the above relationship.

Alternatively, one may say that the predicted values corresponding to the above model, namely

$$\hat{Y}_i = \beta_0 + \beta_1 \phi_1(X_{i1}) + \cdots + \beta_p \phi_p(X_{ip}) \qquad (i = 1, \ldots, n),$$

are linear functions of the β_j.

Given that estimation is undertaken on the basis of a least squares analysis, estimates of the unknown parameters β_j are determined by minimising a sum of squares function

$$S = \sum_{i=1}^{n} \left(Y_i - \beta_0 - \beta_1 \phi_1(X_{i1}) - \cdots - \beta_p \phi_p(X_{ip}) \right)^2 .$$ |
| Decision boundary | In a statistical-classification problem with two classes, a Decision boundary or decision surface is a hypersurface that partitions the underlying vector space into two sets, one for each class. The classifier will classify all the points on one side of the Decision boundary as belonging to one class and all those on the other side as belonging to the other class. |

If the decision surface is a hyperplane, then the classification problem is linear, and the classes are linearly separable.

Parameters

In probability theory, one may describe the distribution of a random variable as belonging to a family of probability distributions, distinguished from each other by the values of a finite number of Parameters. For example, one talks about `a Poisson distribution with mean value λ`. The function defining the distribution (the probability mass function) is:

$$f(k; \lambda) = \frac{e^{-\lambda} \lambda^k}{k!}.$$

This example nicely illustrates the distinction between constants, Parameters, and variables e is Euler`s Number, a fundamental mathematical constant.

Bias

In statistics, Bias is systematic favoritism that is present in the data collection process resulting in misleading results. There are several types of statistical Bias:

· Selection Bias, where there is an error in choosing the individuals or groups to take part in a scientific study. It includes sampling Bias, in which some members of the population are more likely to be included than others. Spectrum Bias consists of evaluating the ability of a diagnostic test in a Biased group of patients, which leads to an overestimate of the sensitivity or specificity of the test. Funding Bias may lead to selection of outcomes, test samples, or test procedures that favor a study`s financial sponsor.

· The Bias of an estimator is the difference between an estimator`s expectation and the true value of the parameter being estimated. Omitted-variable Bias is the Bias that appears in estimates of parameters in a regression analysis when the assumed specification is incorrect, in that it omits an independent variable that should be in the model.

· In statistical hypothesis testing, a test is said to be unBiased when the probability of rejecting the null hypothesis exceeds the significance level when the alternative is true and is less than or equal to the significance level when the null hypothesis is true.

· Systematic Bias or systemic Bias are external influences that may affect the accuracy of statistical measurements.

· Data-snooping Bias comes from the misuse of data mining techniques.

Normal distribution	In probability theory and statistics, the Normal distribution or Gaussian distribution is a continuous probability distribution that describes data that cluster around a mean or average. The graph of the associated probability density function is bell-shaped, with a peak at the mean, and is known as the Gaussian function or bell curve. The Gaussian distribution is one of many things named after Carl Friedrich Gauss, who used it to analyze astronomical data, and determined the formula for its probability density function.
Variance	In probability theory and statistics, the Variance is used as one of several descriptors of a distribution. It describes how far values lie from the mean. In particular, the Variance is one of the moments of a distribution.
Degrees of freedom	In statistics, the number of degrees of freedom is the number of values in the final calculation of a statistic that are free to vary.
	Estimates of statistical parameters can be based upon different amounts of information or data. The number of independent pieces of information that go into the estimate of a parameter is called the degrees of freedom.
Loss function	In statistics, decision theory and economics, a Loss function is a function that maps an event onto a real number representing the economic cost or regret associated with the event.
	More specifically, in statistics a Loss function represents the loss (cost in money or loss in utility in some other sense) associated with an estimate being `wrong` (different from either a desired or a true value) as a function of a measure of the degree of wrongness (generally the difference between the estimated value and the true or desired value).
	Given a random variable X over the probability space $(\mathcal{X}, \Sigma, P_\theta)$ determined by a parameter $\theta \in \Theta$, and a set A of possible actions, a decision rule is a function $\delta : \mathcal{X} \rightarrow A$.
	A Loss function is a real lower-bounded function L on $\Theta \times A$. The value $L(\theta, \delta)$ is the cost of action $\delta(X)$ under parameter θ.

Clam101

Chapter 1. Overview of Supervised Learning

Decision theory	Decision theory in economics, philosophy, mathematics and statistics is concerned with identifying the values, uncertainties and other issues relevant in a given decision, its rationality, and the resulting optimal decision. It is very closely related to the field of game theory.
	Most of Decision theory is normative or prescriptive, i.e., it is concerned with identifying the best decision to take, assuming an ideal decision maker who is fully informed, able to compute with perfect accuracy, and fully rational.
Curse of dimensionality	The Curse of dimensionality is the problem caused by the exponential increase in volume associated with adding extra dimensions to a (mathematical) space. The term was coined by Richard Bellman.
	For example, 100 evenly-spaced sample points suffice to sample a unit interval with no more than 0.01 distance between points; an equivalent sampling of a 10-dimensional unit hypercube with a lattice with a spacing of 0.01 between adjacent points would require 10^{20} sample points: thus, in some sense, the 10-dimensional hypercube can be said to be a factor of 10^{18} `larger` than the unit interval.
Mean	In statistics, mean has two related meanings:
	· the arithmetic mean .
	· the expected value of a random variable, which is also called the population mean. It is sometimes stated that the `mean` means average. This is incorrect if `mean` is taken in the specific sense of `arithmetic mean` as there are different types of averages: the mean, median, and mode.
Mean square error	In statistics, the Mean square error of an estimator is one of many ways to quantify the difference between an estimator and the true value of the quantity being estimated. Mean square error is a risk function, corresponding to the expected value of the squared error loss or quadratic loss. Mean square error measures the average of the square of the `error.` The error is the amount by which the estimator differs from the quantity to be estimated.

Chapter 1. Overview of Supervised Learning

Function approximation	The need for Function approximations arises in many branches of applied mathematics, and computer science in particular. In general, a Function approximation problem asks us to select a function among a well-defined class that closely matches (`approximates`) a target function in a task-specific way.
	One can distinguish two major classes of Function approximation problems: First, for known target functions approximation theory is the branch of numerical analysis that investigates how certain known functions (for example, special functions) can be approximated by a specific class of functions that often have desirable properties (inexpensive computation, continuity, integral and limit values, etc)..
Statistical model	A Statistical model is a set of mathematical equations which describe the behavior of an object of study in terms of random variables and their associated probability distributions. If the model has only one equation it is called a single-equation model, whereas if it has more than one equation, it is known as a multiple-equation model.
	In mathematical terms, a Statistical model is frequently thought of as a pair (Y,P) where Y is the set of possible observations and P the set of possible probability distributions on Y.
Maximum likelihood	Maximum likelihood estimation (MLE) is a popular statistical method used for fitting a statistical model to data, and providing estimates for the model`s parameters.
	The method of Maximum likelihood corresponds to many well-known estimation methods in statistics. For example, suppose you are interested in the heights of adult female giraffes.
Multivariate adaptive regression splines	Multivariate adaptive regression splines is a form of regression analysis introduced by Jerome Friedman in 1991. It is a non-parametric regression technique and can be seen as an extension of linear models that automatically models non-linearities and interactions.
	The term is trademarked and licensed to Salford Systems.

This section introduces Multivariate adaptive regression splines using a few examples. We start with a set of data: a matrix of input variables x, and a vector of the observed responses y, with a response for each row in x. For example, the data could be:

x	y
10.5	16.4
10.7	18.8
10.8	19.7
...	...
20.6	77.0

Here there is only one independent variable, so the x matrix is just a single column. Given these measurements, we would like to build a model which predicts the expected y for a given x.

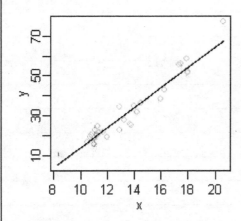

A linear model

A linear model for the above data is

$$\hat{y} = -37 + 5.1x$$

The hat on the $\hat{y}$ indicates that $\hat{y}$ is estimated from the data. The figure on the right shows a plot of this function: a line giving the predicted $\hat{y}$ versus x, with the original values of y shown as red dots.

Smoothing

In statistics and image processing, to smooth a data set is to create an approximating function that attempts to capture important patterns in the data, while leaving out noise or other fine-scale structures/rapid phenomena. Many different algorithms are used in Smoothing. One of the most common algorithms is the `moving average`, often used to try to capture important trends in repeated statistical surveys.

Hat matrix	In statistics, the Hat matrix, H, relates the fitted values to the observed values. It describes the influence each observed value has on each fitted value. The diagonal elements of the Hat matrix are the leverages, which describe the influence each observed value has on the fitted value for that same observation.

If the vector of observed values is denoted by y and the vector of fitted values by Å·,

$$\hat{\mathbf{y}} = H\mathbf{y}.$$

As Å· is usually pronounced `y-hat`, the Hat matrix is so named as it `puts a hat on y`.

Orthogonal	In mathematics, two vectors are Orthogonal if they are perpendicular, i.e., they form a right angle. The word comes from the Greek á½€ρθÏŒς , meaning `straight`, and γωνÎ α (gonia), meaning `angle`.

· Two vectors x and y in an inner product space V are Orthogonal if their inner product $\langle x, y \rangle$ is zero. This situation is denoted $x \perp y$.

· Two vector subspaces A and B of an inner product space V are called Orthogonal subspaces if each vector in A is Orthogonal to each vector in B.

QR decomposition	In linear algebra, a QR decomposition of a matrix is a decomposition of the matrix into an orthogonal and an upper triangular matrix. QR decomposition is often used to solve the linear least squares problem, and is the basis for a particular eigenvalue algorithm, the QR algorithm.

Any real square matrix A may be decomposed as

$$A = QR,$$

where Q is an orthogonal matrix (its columns are orthogonal unit vectors meaning $Q^{T}Q = I$) and R is an upper triangular matrix (also called right triangular matrix).

Chapter 2. Linear Methods for Regression

Model selection	Model selection is the task of selecting a statistical model from a set of potential models, given data. In the simplest cases, a pre-existing set of data is considered. However the task can also involve the design of experiments such that the data collected is well-suited to the problem of Model selection.
	In its most basic forms, Model selection is one of the fundamental tasks of scientific inquiry. Determining the principle that explains a series of observations is often linked directly to a mathematical model predicting those observations. For example, when Galileo performed his inclined plane experiments, he demonstrated that the motion of the balls fitted the parabola predicted by his model.
Subset	In mathematics, especially in set theory, a set A is a subset of a set B if A is `contained` inside B. Notice that A and B may coincide. The relationship of one set being a subset of another is called inclusion.

If A and B are sets and every element of A is also an element of B, then:

· A is a subset of (or is included in) B, denoted by $A \subseteq B$,

or equivalently

· B is a superset of (or includes) A, denoted by $B \supseteq A$.

If A is a subset of B, but A is not equal to B (i.e. there exists at least one element of B not contained in A), then

· A is also a proper (or strict) subset of B; this is written as $A \subsetneq B$.

or equivalently

· B is a proper superset of A; this is written as $B \supsetneq A$.

For any set S, the inclusion relation $\subseteq$ is a partial order on the set 2^S of all subset s of S (the power set of S.)

Chapter 2. Linear Methods for Regression

Some authors use the symbols ⊂ and ⊃ to indicate subset and `superset` respectively, instead of the symbols ⊆ and ⊇, but with the same meaning.

Forward selection	In stepwise regression Forward selection involves starting with no variables in the model, trying out the variables one by one and including them if they are `statistically significant`. Usually, this takes the form of a sequence of F-tests, but other techniques are possible, such as t-tests, adjusted R-square, Akaike information criterion, Bayesian information criterion, Mallows` Cp, or false discovery rate.
Stepwise selection	Stepwise selection is a method that allows moves in either direction, dropping or adding variables at the various steps. It is usually apply in a forward or backward way. The process is one of alternation between choosing the least significant variable to drop and then re-considering all dropped variables for re-introduction into the model.
Singular value decomposition	In linear algebra, the Singular value decomposition is an important factorization of a rectangular real or complex matrix, with many applications in signal processing and statistics. Applications which employ the Singular value decomposition include computing the pseudoinverse, least squares fitting of data, matrix approximation, and determining the rank, range and null space of a matrix.
	Suppose M is an m×n matrix whose entries come from the field K, which is either the field of real numbers or the field of complex numbers. Then there exists a factorization of the form

$$M = U \Sigma V^*,$$

	where U is an m×m unitary matrix over K, the matrix Σ is an m×n diagonal matrix with nonnegative real numbers on the diagonal, and V* denotes the conjugate transpose of V, an n×n unitary matrix over K. Such a factorization is called the singular-value decomposition of M.
Inductive reasoning	Inductive reasoning is a kind of reasoning that allows for the possibility that the conclusion is false even where all of the premises are true. The premises of an inductive logical argument indicate some degree of support for the conclusion but do not entail it; i.e. they do not ensure its truth. Induction is employed, for example, in the following argument:
	All of the ice we have examined so far is cold.

	Therefore, all ice is cold
Degrees of freedom	In statistics, the number of degrees of freedom is the number of values in the final calculation of a statistic that are free to vary.
	Estimates of statistical parameters can be based upon different amounts of information or data. The number of independent pieces of information that go into the estimate of a parameter is called the degrees of freedom.
Additive model	In statistics, an Additive model is a nonparametric regression method. It was suggested by Jerome H. Friedman and Werner Stuetzle (1981) and is an essential part of the ACE algorithm. The Additive model uses a one dimensional smoother to build a restricted class of nonparametric regression models. Because of this, it is less affected by the curse of dimensionality than e.g. a p-dimensional smoother. Furthermore, the Additive model is more flexible than a standard linear model, while being more interpretable than a general regression surface at the cost of approximation errors. Problems with Additive model include model selection, overfitting, and multicollinearity.

Given a data set $\{y_i, x_{i1}, \ldots, x_{ip}\}_{i=1}^n$ of n statistical units, where $\{x_{i1}, \ldots, x_{ip}\}_{i=1}^n$ represent predictors and y_i is the outcome, the Additive model takes the form

$$E[y_i|x_{i1}, \ldots, x_{ip}] = \sum_{j=1}^p f_j(x_{ij})$$

or

$$Y = \beta_0 + \sum_{j=1}^p f_j(X_j) + \varepsilon$$

Where $E[\varepsilon] = 0$, $\text{Var}(\varepsilon) = \sigma^2$ and $E[f_j(X_j)] = 0$. The functions $f_j(x_{ij})$ are unknown smooth functions fit from the data. Fitting the Additive model (i.e. the functions f_j) can be done using the backfitting algorithm proposed by Andreas Buja, Trevor Hastie and Robert Tibshirani (1989).

Chapter 2. Linear Methods for Regression

Parameters	In probability theory, one may describe the distribution of a random variable as belonging to a family of probability distributions, distinguished from each other by the values of a finite number of Parameters. For example, one talks about `a Poisson distribution with mean value λ`. The function defining the distribution (the probability mass function) is:

$$f(k; \lambda) = \frac{e^{-\lambda}\lambda^k}{k!}.$$

This example nicely illustrates the distinction between constants, Parameters, and variables e is Euler`s Number, a fundamental mathematical constant. |
| Partial least squares regression | Partial least squares regression is a statistical method that bears some relation to principal components regression; instead of finding hyperplanes of maximum variance between the response and independent variables, it finds a linear regression model by projecting the predicted variables and the observable variables to a new space. Because both the X and Y data are projected to new spaces, the PLS family of methods are known as bilinear factor models. Partial least squares Discriminant Analysis (PLS-DA)

It is used to find the fundamental relations between two matrices (X and Y), i.e. a latent variable approach to modeling the covariance structures in these two spaces. A PLS model will try to find the multidimensional direction in the X space that explains the maximum multidimensional variance direction in the Y space. PLS-regression is particularly suited when the matrix of predictors has more variables than observations, and when there is multicollinearity among X values. By contrast, standard regression will fail in these cases.
The general underlying model of multivariate PLS is

$$X = TP^T + E$$
$$Y = TQ^T + F,$$

where X is an $n \times m$ matrix of predictors, Y is an $n \times p$ matrix of responses, T is an $n \times l$ matrix (the score, component or factor matrix), P and Q are, respectively, $m \times l$ and $p \times l$ loading matrices, and matrices E and F are the error terms, assumed to be i.i.d. normal. |

Chapter 3. Linear Methods for Classification

Linear regression	In statistics, Linear regression is any approach to modeling the relationship between a scalar variable y and one or more variables denoted X. In Linear regression, models of the unknown parameters are estimated from the data using linear functions. Such models are called `linear models.` Most commonly, Linear regression refers to a model in which the conditional mean of y given the value of X is an affine function of X. Less commonly, Linear regression could refer to a model in which the median, or some other quantile of the conditional distribution of y given X is expressed as a linear function of X. Like all forms of regression analysis, Linear regression focuses on the conditional probability distribution of y given X, rather than on the joint probability distribution of y and X, which is the domain of multivariate analysis. Linear regression was the first type of regression analysis to be studied rigorously, and to be used extensively in practical applications.
Naive Bayes classifier	A Bayes classifier is a simple probabilistic classifier based on applying Bayes` theorem (from Bayesian statistics) with strong (naive) independence assumptions. A more descriptive term for the underlying probability model would be `independent feature model`. In simple terms, a Naive Bayes classifier assumes that the presence (or absence) of a particular feature of a class is unrelated to the presence (or absence) of any other feature.
Linear discriminant analysis	Linear discriminant analysis and the related Fisher`s linear discriminant are methods used in statistics, pattern recognition and machine learning to find a linear combination of features which characterize or separate two or more classes of objects or events. The resulting combination may be used as a linear classifier, or, more commonly, for dimensionality reduction before later classification. Linear discriminant analysis is closely related to ANOVA (analysis of variance) and regression analysis, which also attempt to express one dependent variable as a linear combination of other features or measurements. In the other two methods however, the dependent variable is a numerical quantity, while for Linear discriminant analysis it is a categorical variable (i.e. the class label). Logistic regression and probit regression are more similar to Linear discriminant analysis, as they also explain a categorical variable. These other methods are preferable in applications where it is not reasonable to assume that the independent variables are normally distributed, which is a fundamental assumption of the Linear discriminant analysis method.

Variance	In probability theory and statistics, the Variance is used as one of several descriptors of a distribution. It describes how far values lie from the mean. In particular, the Variance is one of the moments of a distribution.
Covariance	In probability theory and statistics, covariance is a measure of how much two variables change together. (Variance is a special case of the covariance when the two variables are identical). The covariance between two real-valued random variables X and Y, with expected values $E(X) = \mu$ and $E(Y) = \nu$ is defined as

$$\mathrm{Cov}(X, Y) = \mathrm{E}((X - \mu)(Y - \nu)),$$

where E is the expected value operator. |
| Covariance matrix | If the entries in the column vector

$$\mathbf{X} = \begin{bmatrix} X_1 \\ \vdots \\ X_n \end{bmatrix}$$

are random variables, each with finite variance, then the Covariance matrix Σ is the matrix whose (i, j) entry is the covariance

$$\Sigma_{ij} = \mathrm{cov}(X_i, X_j) = \mathrm{E}\big[(X_i - \mu_i)(X_j - \mu_j)\big]$$

where

$$\mu_i = \mathrm{E}(X_i)$$ |

is the expected value of the ith entry in the vector X. In other words, we have

$$\Sigma = \begin{bmatrix} \mathrm{E}[(X_1 - \mu_1)(X_1 - \mu_1)] & \mathrm{E}[(X_1 - \mu_1)(X_2 - \mu_2)] & \cdots & \mathrm{E}[(X_1 - \mu_1)(X_n - \mu_n)] \\ \mathrm{E}[(X_2 - \mu_2)(X_1 - \mu_1)] & \mathrm{E}[(X_2 - \mu_2)(X_2 - \mu_2)] & \cdots & \mathrm{E}[(X_2 - \mu_2)(X_n - \mu_n)] \\ \vdots & \vdots & \ddots & \vdots \\ \mathrm{E}[(X_n - \mu_n)(X_1 - \mu_1)] & \mathrm{E}[(X_n - \mu_n)(X_2 - \mu_2)] & \cdots & \mathrm{E}[(X_n - \mu_n)(X_n - \mu_n)] \end{bmatrix}.$$

The inverse of this matrix, Σ^{-1}, is the inverse Covariance matrix, aka the concentration matrix or precision matrix. The elements of the precision matrix have an interpretation in terms of partial correlations and partial variances.

The definition above is equivalent to the matrix equality

$$\Sigma = \mathrm{E}\left[(\mathbf{X} - \mathrm{E}[\mathbf{X}])\,(\mathbf{X} - \mathrm{E}[\mathbf{X}])^\top\right]$$

This form can be seen as a generalization of the scalar-valued variance to higher dimensions.

Rayleigh quotient

In mathematics, for a given complex Hermitian matrix A and nonzero vector x, the Rayleigh quotient R(A,x), is defined as :

$$\frac{x^* A x}{x^* x}.$$

For real matrices and vectors, the condition of being Hermitian reduces to that of being symmetric, and the conjugate transpose x* to the usual transpose x`. Note that R(A,cx) = R(A,x) for any real scalar c. Recall that a Hermitian (or real symmetric) matrix has real eigenvalues.

Chapter 3. Linear Methods for Classification

Logistic regression	In statistics, Logistic regression is used for prediction of the probability of occurrence of an event by fitting data to a logit function logistic curve. It is a generalized linear model used for binomial regression. Like many forms of regression analysis, it makes use of several predictor variables that may be either numerical or categorical. An explanation of Logistic regression begins with an explanation of the logistic function: $$f(z) = \frac{e^z}{e^z + 1} = \frac{1}{1 + e^{-z}}$$
Logit	The Logit function is the inverse of the `sigmoid`, or `logistic` function used in mathematics, especially in statistics. Logit is pronounced /ˈloʊdʒɪt/ . The Logit of a number p between 0 and 1 is given by the formula: $$\operatorname{logit}(p) = \log\left(\frac{p}{1-p}\right) = \log(p) - \log(1-p).$$ The base of the logarithm function used is of little importance in the present article, as long as it is greater than 1, but the natural logarithm with base e is the one most often used.
Multinomial distribution	In probability theory, the Multinomial distribution is a generalization of the binomial distribution. The binomial distribution is the probability distribution of the number of `successes` in n independent Bernoulli trials, with the same probability of `success` on each trial. In a Multinomial distribution, the analog of the Bernoulli distribution is the categorical distribution, where each trial results in exactly one of some fixed finite number k of possible outcomes, with probabilities p_1, .. p_k , and there are n independent trials.

Score	In statistics, the Score or Score function is the partial derivative, with respect to some parameter θ, of the logarithm (commonly the natural logarithm) of the likelihood function. If the observation is X and its likelihood is L(θ;X), then the Score V can be found through the chain rule:

$$V = \frac{\partial}{\partial \theta} \log L(\theta; X) = \frac{1}{L(\theta; X)} \frac{\partial L(\theta; X)}{\partial \theta}.$$

Note that V is a function of θ and the observation X, so that, in general, it is not a statistic. Note also that V indicates the sensitivity of L(θ;X) (its variation normalized by its value.)

Hessian matrix	In mathematics, the Hessian matrix is the square matrix of second-order partial derivatives of a function; that is, it describes the local curvature of a function of many variables. The Hessian matrix was developed in the 19th century by the German mathematician Ludwig Otto Hesse and later named after him. Hesse himself had used the term `functional determinants`.
Risk factor	A Risk factor is a variable associated with an increased risk of disease or infection. Risk factor s are correlational and not necessarily causal, because correlation does not imply causation. For example, being young cannot be said to cause measles, but young people are more at risk as they are less likely to have developed immunity during a previous epidemic.
Generalized linear model	In statistics, the Generalized linear model is a flexible generalization of ordinary least squares regression. The Generalized linear model generalizes linear regression by allowing the linear model to be related to the response variable via a link function and by allowing the magnitude of the variance of each measurement to be a function of its predicted value.
	Generalized linear models were formulated by John Nelder and Robert Wedderburn as a way of unifying various other statistical models, including linear regression, logistic regression and Poisson regression.
Wald test	The Wald test is a parametric statistical test named after Abraham Wald with a great variety of uses. Whenever a relationship within or between data items can be expressed as a statistical model with parameters to be estimated from a sample, the Wald test can be used to test the true value of the parameter based on the sample estimate. A Wald test can be used in a great variety of different models including models for dichotomous variables and models for continuous variables.
	Mathematical details

Under the Wald statistical test, the maximum likelihood estimate $\hat{\theta}$ of the parameter(s) of interest θ is compared with the proposed value θ_0, with the assumption that the difference between the two will be approximately normal. Typically the square of the difference is compared to a chi-squared distribution. In the univariate case, the Wald statistic is

$$\frac{(\hat{\theta} - \theta_0)^2}{\mathrm{var}(\hat{\theta})}$$

which is compared against a chi-square distribution.

Score test

A Score test is a statistical test of a simple null hypothesis that a parameter of interest θ is equal to some particular value θ_0. It is the most powerful test when the true value of θ is close to θ_0.

Let L be the likelihood function which depends on a univariate parameter θ and let x be the data. The score is U(θ) where

$$U(\theta) = \frac{\partial \log L(\theta|x)}{\partial \theta}.$$

The observed Fisher information is,

$$I(\theta) = -\frac{\partial^2 \log L(\theta|x)}{\partial \theta^2}.$$

The statistic to test $H_0 : \theta = \theta_0$ is

$$S(\theta) = \frac{U(\theta_0)^2}{I(\theta_0)}$$

which takes a χ_1^2 distribution asymptotically when H_0 is true.

Smoothing

In statistics and image processing, to smooth a data set is to create an approximating function that attempts to capture important patterns in the data, while leaving out noise or other fine-scale structures/rapid phenomena. Many different algorithms are used in Smoothing. One of the most common algorithms is the `moving average`, often used to try to capture important trends in repeated statistical surveys.

Smoothing spline

The Smoothing spline is a method of smoothing (fitting a smooth curve to a set of noisy observations) using a spline function.

Let $(x_i, Y_i); i = 1, \ldots, n$ be a sequence of observations, modeled by the relation $E(Y_i)$ = $\mu(x_i)$. The Smoothing spline estimate $\hat{\mu}$ of the function μ is defined to be the minimizer (over the class of twice differentiable functions) of

$$\sum_{i=1}^{n} (Y_i - \hat{\mu}(x_i))^2 + \lambda \int \hat{\mu}''(x)^2 \, dx.$$

Remarks:

· $\lambda \geq 0$ is a smoothing parameter, controlling the trade-off between fidelity to the data and roughness of the function estimate.

· The integral is evaluated over the range of the x_i.

· As $\lambda \rightarrow 0$ (no smoothing), the Smoothing spline converges to the interpolating spline.

· As $\lambda \rightarrow \infty$, the roughness penalty becomes paramount and the estimate converges to a linear least squares estimate.

· The roughness penalty based on the second derivative is the most common in modern statistics literature, although the method can easily be adapted to penalties based on other derivatives.

· In early literature, with equally-spaced x_i, second or third-order differences were used in the penalty, rather than derivatives.

· When the sum-of-squares term is replaced by a log-likelihood, the resulting estimate is termed penalized likelihood. The Smoothing spline is the special case of penalized likelihood resulting from a Gaussian likelihood

Degrees of freedom

In statistics, the number of degrees of freedom is the number of values in the final calculation of a statistic that are free to vary.

Estimates of statistical parameters can be based upon different amounts of information or data. The number of independent pieces of information that go into the estimate of a parameter is called the degrees of freedom.

Additive model

In statistics, an Additive model is a nonparametric regression method. It was suggested by Jerome H. Friedman and Werner Stuetzle (1981) and is an essential part of the ACE algorithm. The Additive model uses a one dimensional smoother to build a restricted class of nonparametric regression models. Because of this, it is less affected by the curse of dimensionality than e.g. a p-dimensional smoother. Furthermore, the Additive model is more flexible than a standard linear model, while being more interpretable than a general regression surface at the cost of approximation errors. Problems with Additive model include model selection, overfitting, and multicollinearity.

Given a data set $\{y_i, x_{i1}, \ldots, x_{ip}\}_{i=1}^{n}$ of n statistical units, where $\{x_{i1}, \ldots, x_{ip}\}_{i=1}^{n}$ represent predictors and y_i is the outcome, the Additive model takes the form

$$E[y_i | x_{i1}, \ldots, x_{ip}] = \sum_{j=1}^{p} f_j(x_{ij})$$

or

$$Y = \beta_0 + \sum_{j=1}^{p} f_j(X_j) + \varepsilon$$

Where $E[\varepsilon] = 0$, $Var(\varepsilon) = \sigma^2$ and $E[f_j(X_j)] = 0$. The functions $f_j(x_{ij})$ are unknown smooth functions fit from the data. Fitting the Additive model (i.e. the functions f_j) can be done using the backfitting algorithm proposed by Andreas Buja, Trevor Hastie and Robert Tibshirani (1989).

Parameters

In probability theory, one may describe the distribution of a random variable as belonging to a family of probability distributions, distinguished from each other by the values of a finite number of Parameters. For example, one talks about `a Poisson distribution with mean value $\lambda$`. The function defining the distribution (the probability mass function) is:

$$f(k; \lambda) = \frac{e^{-\lambda}\lambda^k}{k!}.$$

This example nicely illustrates the distinction between constants, Parameters, and variables e is Euler`s Number, a fundamental mathematical constant.

Kernel

A Kernel is a weighting function used in non-parametric estimation techniques. Kernels are used in Kernel density estimation to estimate random variables` density functions, or in Kernel regression to estimate the conditional expectation of a random variable. Kernels are also used in time-series, in the use of the periodogram to estimate the spectral density.
A Kernel is a non-negative real-valued integrable function K satisfying the following two requirements:

$$\int_{-\infty}^{+\infty} K(u)\,du = 1\,;$$

$$K(-u) = K(u) \text{ for all values of } u\,.$$

The first requirement ensures that the method of Kernel density estimation results in a probability density function. The second requirement ensures that the average of the corresponding distribution is equal to that of the sample used.

Variance

In probability theory and statistics, the Variance is used as one of several descriptors of a distribution. It describes how far values lie from the mean. In particular, the Variance is one of the moments of a distribution.

Chapter 4. Basis Expansions and Regularization

Bias	In statistics, Bias is systematic favoritism that is present in the data collection process resulting in misleading results. There are several types of statistical Bias:
	· Selection Bias, where there is an error in choosing the individuals or groups to take part in a scientific study. It includes sampling Bias, in which some members of the population are more likely to be included than others. Spectrum Bias consists of evaluating the ability of a diagnostic test in a Biased group of patients, which leads to an overestimate of the sensitivity or specificity of the test. Funding Bias may lead to selection of outcomes, test samples, or test procedures that favor a study`s financial sponsor.
	· The Bias of an estimator is the difference between an estimator`s expectation and the true value of the parameter being estimated. Omitted-variable Bias is the Bias that appears in estimates of parameters in a regression analysis when the assumed specification is incorrect, in that it omits an independent variable that should be in the model.
	· In statistical hypothesis testing, a test is said to be unBiased when the probability of rejecting the null hypothesis exceeds the significance level when the alternative is true and is less than or equal to the significance level when the null hypothesis is true.
	· Systematic Bias or systemic Bias are external influences that may affect the accuracy of statistical measurements.
	· Data-snooping Bias comes from the misuse of data mining techniques.
Hilbert space	The mathematical concept of a Hilbert space generalizes the notion of Euclidean space. It extends the methods of vector algebra and calculus from the two-dimensional Euclidean plane and three-dimensional space to spaces with any finite or infinite number of dimensions. A Hilbert space is an abstract vector space possessing the structure of an inner product that allows length and angle to be measured.
Reproducing kernel Hilbert space	In functional analysis (a branch of mathematics), a Reproducing kernel Hilbert space is a Hilbert space of functions in which pointwise evaluation is a continuous linear functional. Equivalently, they are spaces that can be defined by reproducing kernels. The subject was originally and simultaneously developed by Nachman Aronszajn (1907-1980) and Stefan Bergman (1895-1977) in 1950.

An important subset of the Reproducing kernel Hilbert spaces are the Reproducing kernel Hilbert spaces associated to a continuous kernel. These spaces have wide applications, including complex analysis, quantum mechanics and harmonic analysis.

Let X be an arbitrary set and H a Hilbert space of complex-valued functions on X. We say that H is a Reproducing kernel Hilbert space if every linear map of the form

$$L_x : f \mapsto f(x)$$

from H to the complex numbers is continuous for any x in X. By the Riesz representation theorem, this implies that for every x in X there exists a unique element K_x of H with the property that:

$$f(x) = \langle f,\ K_x \rangle \quad \forall f \in H \quad (*).$$

The function K_x is called the point-evaluation functional at the point x.

Since H is a space of functions, the element K_x is itself a function and can therefore be evaluated at every point. We define the function $K : X \times X \to \mathbb{C}$ by

$$K(x,y) \stackrel{\text{def}}{=} \overline{K_x(y)}.$$

This function is called the reproducing kernel for the Hilbert space H and it is determined entirely by H because the Riesz representation theorem guarantees, for every x in X, that the element K_x satisfying (*) is unique.

Fourier transform

In mathematics, the Fourier transform is an operation that transforms one complex-valued function of a real variable into another. In such applications as signal processing, the domain of the original function is typically time and is accordingly called the time domain. That of the new function is frequency, and so the Fourier transform is often called the frequency domain representation of the original function.

There are several common conventions for defining the Fourier transform of an integrable function $f ≉: R \rightarrow C$ (Kaiser 1994). This article will use the definition:

$$\hat{f}(\xi) = \int_{-\infty}^{\infty} f(x)\, e^{-2\pi i x \xi}\, dx,$$

for every real number ξ.

When the independent variable x represents time (with SI unit of seconds), the transform variable ξ represents frequency (in hertz). Under suitable conditions, f can be reconstructed from $\hat{f}$ by the inverse transform:

$$f(x) = \int_{-\infty}^{\infty} \hat{f}(\xi)\, e^{2\pi i x \xi}\, d\xi,$$

for every real number x.

Kriging

Kriging is a group of geostatistical techniques to interpolate the value of a random field (e.g., the elevation, z, of the landscape as a function of the geographic location) at an unobserved location from observations of its value at nearby locations.

The theory behind interpolation and extrapolation by Kriging was developed by the French mathematician Georges Matheron based on the Master`s thesis of Daniel Gerhardus Krige, the pioneering plotter of distance-weighted average gold grades at the Witwatersrand reef complex in South Africa. The English verb is to krige and the most common noun is Kriging; both are often pronounced with a hard `g`, following the pronunciation of the name `Krige`.

Kriging belongs to the family of linear least squares estimation algorithms.

Polynomial regression

In statistics, Polynomial regression is a form of linear regression in which the relationship between the independent variable x and the dependent variable y is modeled as an nth order polynomial. Polynomial regression fits a nonlinear relationship between the value of x and the corresponding conditional mean of y, denoted E, and has been used to describe nonlinear phenomena such as the growth rate of tissues, the distribution of carbon isotopes in lake sediments , and the progression of disease epidemics. Although Polynomial regression fits a nonlinear model to the data, as a statistical estimation problem it is linear, in the sense that the regression function E is linear in the unknown parameters that are estimated from the data.

Polynomial regression models are usually fit using the method of least squares. The least-squares method minimizes the variance of the unbiased estimators of the coefficients, under the conditions of the Gauss-Markov theorem. The least-squares method was published in 1805 by Legendre and in 1809 by Gauss. The first design of an experiment for Polynomial regression appeared in an 1815 paper of Gergonne. In the twentieth century, Polynomial regression played an important role in the development of regression analysis, with a greater emphasis on issues of design and inference. More recently, the use of polynomial models has been complemented by other methods, with non-polynomial models having advantages for some classes of problems. The goal of regression analysis is to model the expected value of a dependent variable y in terms of the value of an independent variable (or vector of independent variables) x. In simple linear regression, the model

$$y = a_0 + a_1 x + \varepsilon,$$

is used, where ε is an unobserved random error with mean zero conditioned on a scalar variable x. In this model, for each unit increase in the value of x, the conditional expectation of y increases by a_1 units.

Singular value decomposition

In linear algebra, the Singular value decomposition is an important factorization of a rectangular real or complex matrix, with many applications in signal processing and statistics. Applications which employ the Singular value decomposition include computing the pseudoinverse, least squares fitting of data, matrix approximation, and determining the rank, range and null space of a matrix.

Suppose M is an m×n matrix whose entries come from the field K, which is either the field of real numbers or the field of complex numbers. Then there exists a factorization of the form

$$M = U\Sigma V^*,$$

where U is an m×m unitary matrix over K, the matrix Σ is an m×n diagonal matrix with nonnegative real numbers on the diagonal, and V* denotes the conjugate transpose of V, an n×n unitary matrix over K. Such a factorization is called the singular-value decomposition of M.

Chapter 4. Basis Expansions and Regularization

Multiresolution analysis	A Multiresolution analysis or multiscale approximation (MSA) is the design method of most of the practically relevant discrete wavelet transforms (DWT) and the justification for the algorithm of the fast wavelet transform (FWT). It was introduced in this context in 1988/89 by Stephane Mallat and Yves Meyer and has predecessors in the microlocal analysis in the theory of differential equations (the ironing method) and the pyramid methods of image processing as introduced in 1981/83 by Peter J. Burt, Edward H. Adelson and James Crowley.

A Multiresolution analysis of the space $L^2(\mathbb{R})$ consists of a sequence of nested subspaces

$$\{0\} \cdots \subset V_0 \subset V_1 \subset \cdots \subset V_n \subset V_{n+1} \subset \cdots \subset L^2(\mathbb{R})$$

that satisfies certain self-similarity relations in time/space and scale/frequency, as well as completeness and regularity relations.

B-Spline	In the mathematical subfield of numerical analysis, a B-spline is a spline function that has minimal support with respect to a given degree, smoothness, and domain partition. A fundamental theorem states that every spline function of a given degree, smoothness, and domain partition, can be represented as a linear combination of B-splines of that same degree and smoothness, and over that same partition. The term B-spline was coined by Isaac Jacob Schoenberg and is short for basis spline.

Chapter 5. Kernel Smoothing Methods

LOESS	LOESS, or LOWESS (locally weighted scatterplot smoothing), is one of many `modern` modeling methods that build on `classical` methods, such as linear and nonlinear least squares regression. Modern regression methods are designed to address situations in which the classical procedures do not perform well or cannot be effectively applied without undue labor. LOESS combines much of the simplicity of linear least squares regression with the flexibility of nonlinear regression.
Polynomial regression	In statistics, Polynomial regression is a form of linear regression in which the relationship between the independent variable x and the dependent variable y is modeled as an nth order polynomial. Polynomial regression fits a nonlinear relationship between the value of x and the corresponding conditional mean of y, denoted E, and has been used to describe nonlinear phenomena such as the growth rate of tissues, the distribution of carbon isotopes in lake sediments , and the progression of disease epidemics. Although Polynomial regression fits a nonlinear model to the data, as a statistical estimation problem it is linear, in the sense that the regression function E is linear in the unknown parameters that are estimated from the data.

Polynomial regression models are usually fit using the method of least squares. The least-squares method minimizes the variance of the unbiased estimators of the coefficients, under the conditions of the Gauss-Markov theorem. The least-squares method was published in 1805 by Legendre and in 1809 by Gauss. The first design of an experiment for Polynomial regression appeared in an 1815 paper of Gergonne. In the twentieth century, Polynomial regression played an important role in the development of regression analysis, with a greater emphasis on issues of design and inference. More recently, the use of polynomial models has been complemented by other methods, with non-polynomial models having advantages for some classes of problems. The goal of regression analysis is to model the expected value of a dependent variable y in terms of the value of an independent variable (or vector of independent variables) x. In simple linear regression, the model

$$y = a_0 + a_1 x + \varepsilon,$$

is used, where ε is an unobserved random error with mean zero conditioned on a scalar variable x. In this model, for each unit increase in the value of x, the conditional expectation of y increases by a_1 units.

Chapter 5. Kernel Smoothing Methods

Smoothing	In statistics and image processing, to smooth a data set is to create an approximating function that attempts to capture important patterns in the data, while leaving out noise or other fine-scale structures/rapid phenomena. Many different algorithms are used in Smoothing. One of the most common algorithms is the `moving average`, often used to try to capture important trends in repeated statistical surveys.
Parameters	In probability theory, one may describe the distribution of a random variable as belonging to a family of probability distributions, distinguished from each other by the values of a finite number of Parameters. For example, one talks about `a Poisson distribution with mean value λ`. The function defining the distribution (the probability mass function) is: $$f(k; \lambda) = \frac{e^{-\lambda}\lambda^k}{k!}.$$ This example nicely illustrates the distinction between constants, Parameters, and variables e is Euler`s Number, a fundamental mathematical constant.
Density estimation	In probability and statistics, Density estimation is the construction of an estimate, based on observed data, of an unobservable underlying probability density function. The unobservable density function is thought of as the density according to which a large population is distributed; the data are usually thought of as a random sample from that population. A variety of approaches to Density estimation are used, including Parzen windows and a range of data clustering techniques, including vector quantization.
Kernel	A Kernel is a weighting function used in non-parametric estimation techniques. Kernels are used in Kernel density estimation to estimate random variables` density functions, or in Kernel regression to estimate the conditional expectation of a random variable. Kernels are also used in time-series, in the use of the periodogram to estimate the spectral density. A Kernel is a non-negative real-valued integrable function K satisfying the following two requirements: $$\int_{-\infty}^{+\infty} K(u)\,du = 1\,;$$

$$. \ K(-u) = K(u) \text{ for all values of } u.$$

The first requirement ensures that the method of Kernel density estimation results in a probability density function. The second requirement ensures that the average of the corresponding distribution is equal to that of the sample used.

Naive Bayes classifier

A Bayes classifier is a simple probabilistic classifier based on applying Bayes` theorem (from Bayesian statistics) with strong (naive) independence assumptions. A more descriptive term for the underlying probability model would be `independent feature model`.

In simple terms, a Naive Bayes classifier assumes that the presence (or absence) of a particular feature of a class is unrelated to the presence (or absence) of any other feature.

Radial basis function

A Radial basis function is a real-valued function whose value depends only on the distance from the origin, so that $\phi(\mathbf{x}) = \phi(\|\mathbf{x}\|)$ or alternatively on the distance from some other point c, called a center, so that $\phi(\mathbf{x}, \mathbf{c}) = \phi(\|\mathbf{x} - \mathbf{c}\|)$. Any function φ that satisfies the property $\phi(\mathbf{x}) = \phi(\|\mathbf{x}\|)$ is a radial function. The norm is usually Euclidean distance, although other distance functions are also possible.

Bias	In statistics, Bias is systematic favoritism that is present in the data collection process resulting in misleading results. There are several types of statistical Bias:
	· Selection Bias, where there is an error in choosing the individuals or groups to take part in a scientific study. It includes sampling Bias, in which some members of the population are more likely to be included than others. Spectrum Bias consists of evaluating the ability of a diagnostic test in a Biased group of patients, which leads to an overestimate of the sensitivity or specificity of the test. Funding Bias may lead to selection of outcomes, test samples, or test procedures that favor a study's financial sponsor.
	· The Bias of an estimator is the difference between an estimator's expectation and the true value of the parameter being estimated. Omitted-variable Bias is the Bias that appears in estimates of parameters in a regression analysis when the assumed specification is incorrect, in that it omits an independent variable that should be in the model.
	· In statistical hypothesis testing, a test is said to be unBiased when the probability of rejecting the null hypothesis exceeds the significance level when the alternative is true and is less than or equal to the significance level when the null hypothesis is true.
	· Systematic Bias or systemic Bias are external influences that may affect the accuracy of statistical measurements.
	· Data-snooping Bias comes from the misuse of data mining techniques.
Loss function	In statistics, decision theory and economics, a Loss function is a function that maps an event onto a real number representing the economic cost or regret associated with the event.
	More specifically, in statistics a Loss function represents the loss (cost in money or loss in utility in some other sense) associated with an estimate being `wrong` (different from either a desired or a true value) as a function of a measure of the degree of wrongness (generally the difference between the estimated value and the true or desired value).

Chapter 6. Model Assessment and Selection

Given a random variable X over the probability space $(\mathcal{X}, \Sigma, P_\theta)$ determined by a parameter $\theta \in \Theta$, and a set A of possible actions, a decision rule is a function $\delta : \mathcal{X} \to A$.

A Loss function is a real lower-bounded function L on $\Theta \times A$. The value $L(\theta, \delta)$ is the cost of action $\delta(X)$ under parameter θ.

Training set

A Training set is a set of data used in various areas of information science to discover potentially predictive relationships. Training sets are used in artificial intelligence, machine learning, genetic programming, intelligent systems, and statistics. In all these fields, a Training set has much the same role and is often used in conjunction with a test set.

Variance

In probability theory and statistics, the Variance is used as one of several descriptors of a distribution. It describes how far values lie from the mean. In particular, the Variance is one of the moments of a distribution.

Overfitting

In statistics, Overfitting occurs when a statistical model describes random error or noise instead of the underlying relationship. Overfitting generally occurs when a model is excessively complex, such as having too many degrees of freedom, in relation to the amount of data available. A model which has been overfit will generally have poor predictive performance, as it can exaggerate minor fluctuations in the data.

Test set

A Test set is a set of data used in various areas of information science to assess the strength and utility of a predictive relationship. Test sets are used in artificial intelligence, machine learning, genetic programming, intelligent systems, and statistics. In all these fields, a Test set has much the same role.

Model selection

Model selection is the task of selecting a statistical model from a set of potential models, given data. In the simplest cases, a pre-existing set of data is considered. However the task can also involve the design of experiments such that the data collected is well-suited to the problem of Model selection.

In its most basic forms, Model selection is one of the fundamental tasks of scientific inquiry. Determining the principle that explains a series of observations is often linked directly to a mathematical model predicting those observations. For example, when Galileo performed his inclined plane experiments, he demonstrated that the motion of the balls fitted the parabola predicted by his model.

Iteratively reweighted least squares

The method of Iteratively reweighted least squares is used to solve certain optimization problems. It solves objective functions of the form:

$$\underset{\boldsymbol{\beta}}{\arg\min} \sum_{i=1}^{n} w_i(\boldsymbol{\beta}) \big| y_i - f_i(\boldsymbol{\beta}) \big|^2,$$

by an iterative method in which each step involves solving a weighted least squares problem of the form:

$$\boldsymbol{\beta}^{(t+1)} = \underset{\boldsymbol{\beta}}{\arg\min} \sum_{i=1}^{n} w_i(\boldsymbol{\beta}^{(t)}) \big| y_i - f_i(\boldsymbol{\beta}) \big|^2.$$

IRLS is used to find the maximum likelihood estimates of a generalized linear model, and in robust regression to find an M-estimator, as a way of mitigating the influence of outliers in an otherwise normally-distributed data set. For example, by minimizing the least absolute error rather than the least square error.

Expectation-maximization

In statistics, an Expectation-maximization algorithm is a method for finding maximum likelihood estimates of parameters in statistical models, where the model depends on unobserved latent variables. expectation maximization is an iterative method which alternates between performing an expectation (E) step, which computes the expectation of the log-likelihood evaluated using the current estimate for the latent variables, and a maximization (M) step, which computes parameters maximizing the expected log-likelihood found on the E step. These parameter-estimates are then used to determine the distribution of the latent variables in the next E step. Given a likelihood function L(θ; x, z), where θ is the parameter vector, x is the observed data and z represents the unobserved latent data or missing values, the maximum likelihood estimate (MLE) is determined by the marginal likelihood of the observed data L(θ; x), however this quantity is often intractable.

The Expectation maximization algorithm seeks to find the MLE of the marginal likelihood by iteratively applying the following two steps:

Expectation step: Calculate the expected value of the log likelihood function, with respect to the conditional distribution of z given x under the current estimate of the parameters $\theta^{(t)}$:

$$Q(\theta|\theta^{(t)}) = \mathrm{E}_{Z|x,\theta^{(t)}} \left[\log L(\theta; x, Z) \right]$$

Maximization step: Find the parameter that maximizes this quantity:

$$\theta^{(t+1)} = \arg\max_{\theta} Q(\theta|\theta^{(t)})$$

Akaike information criterion	Akaike information criterion, developed by Hirotsugu Akaike under the name of `an information criterion` in 1971 and proposed in Akaike (1974), is a measure of the goodness of fit of an estimated statistical model. It is grounded in the concept of entropy, in effect offering a relative measure of the information lost when a given model is used to describe reality and can be said to describe the tradeoff between bias and variance in model construction, or loosely speaking that of precision and complexity of the model.
	The Akaike information criterion is not a test of the model in the sense of hypothesis testing, rather it is a test between models - a tool for model selection.
Sample	In statistics, a Sample is a subset of a population. Typically, the population is very large, making a census or a complete enumeration of all the values in the population impractical or impossible. The Sample represents a subset of manageable size.
Degrees of freedom	In statistics, the number of degrees of freedom is the number of values in the final calculation of a statistic that are free to vary.
	Estimates of statistical parameters can be based upon different amounts of information or data. The number of independent pieces of information that go into the estimate of a parameter is called the degrees of freedom.
Parameters	In probability theory, one may describe the distribution of a random variable as belonging to a family of probability distributions, distinguished from each other by the values of a finite number of Parameters. For example, one talks about `a Poisson distribution with mean value λ`. The function defining the distribution (the probability mass function) is:

$$f(k; \lambda) = \frac{e^{-\lambda}\lambda^k}{k!}.$$

This example nicely illustrates the distinction between constants, Parameters, and variables e is Euler`s Number, a fundamental mathematical constant.

Chapter 6. Model Assessment and Selection

Bayesian information criterion	In statistics, the Bayesian information criterion or Schwarz Criterion is a criterion for model selection among a class of parametric models with different numbers of parameters. Choosing a model to optimize Bayesian information criterion is a form of regularization. When estimating model parameters using maximum likelihood estimation, it is possible to increase the likelihood by adding parameters, which may result in overfitting.
Minimum description length	The Minimum description length principle is a formalization of Occam`s Razor in which the best hypothesis for a given set of data is the one that leads to the best compression of the data. Minimum description length was introduced by Jorma Rissanen in 1978. It is an important concept in information theory and learning theory. Any set of data can be represented by a string of symbols from a finite (say, binary) alphabet.
Information theory	Information theory is a branch of applied mathematics and electrical engineering involving the quantification of information. Information theory was developed by Claude E. Shannon to find fundamental limits on signal processing operations such as compressing data and on reliably storing and communicating data. Since its inception it has broadened to find applications in many other areas, including statistical inference, natural language processing, cryptography generally, networks other than communication networks -- as in neurobiology, the evolution and function of molecular codes, model selection in ecology, thermal physics, quantum computing, plagiarism detection and other forms of data analysis.
Monte Carlo methods	Monte Carlo methods are a class of computational algorithms that rely on repeated random sampling to compute their results. Monte Carlo methods are often used in simulating physical and mathematical systems. Because of their reliance on repeated computation of random or pseudo-random numbers, these methods are most suited to calculation by a computer and tend to be used when it is unfeasible or impossible to compute an exact result with a deterministic algorithm.

CLAM\101

Chapter 7. Model Inference and Averaging

Maximum likelihood	Maximum likelihood estimation (MLE) is a popular statistical method used for fitting a statistical model to data, and providing estimates for the model's parameters.
	The method of Maximum likelihood corresponds to many well-known estimation methods in statistics. For example, suppose you are interested in the heights of adult female giraffes.
Multivariate adaptive regression splines	Multivariate adaptive regression splines is a form of regression analysis introduced by Jerome Friedman in 1991. It is a non-parametric regression technique and can be seen as an extension of linear models that automatically models non-linearities and interactions.
	The term is trademarked and licensed to Salford Systems.
	This section introduces Multivariate adaptive regression splines using a few examples. We start with a set of data: a matrix of input variables x, and a vector of the observed responses y, with a response for each row in x. For example, the data could be:

x   y
10.5 16.4
10.7 18.8
10.8 19.7
...   ...
20.6 77.0

Here there is only one independent variable, so the x matrix is just a single column. Given these measurements, we would like to build a model which predicts the expected y for a given x.

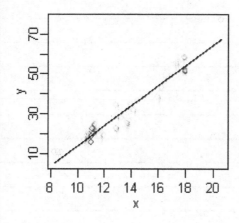

A linear model

A linear model for the above data is

$$\hat{y} = -37 + 5.1x$$

The hat on the $\hat{y}$ indicates that $\hat{y}$ is estimated from the data. The figure on the right shows a plot of this function: a line giving the predicted $\hat{y}$ versus x, with the original values of y shown as red dots.

Likelihood function

In statistics, the Likelihood function is a function of the parameters of a statistical model that plays a key role in statistical inference. In non-technical parlance, `likelihood` is usually a synonym for `probability,` but in statistical usage there is a clear distinction in perspective: the number that is the probability of some observed outcomes given a set of parameter values is regarded as the likelihood of the set of parameter values given the observed outcomes. Mathematically, writing X for the set of observed data and Θ for the set of parameter values, the expression P, the probability of X given Θ, can be interpreted as the expression L, the likelihood of Θ given X. The interpretation of L as a function of Θ is especially obvious when X is fixed and Θ is allowed to vary.

Generally, L is permitted to be any positive multiple of P. More precisely then, a Likelihood function is any representative from an equivalence class of functions,

$$L(\Theta \mid X) \in \{\alpha\, P(X \mid \Theta) : \alpha > 0\} \,,$$

where the constant of proportionality $\alpha > 0$ is not permitted to depend upon Θ. In particular, the numerical value L alone is immaterial; all that matters are likelihood ratios, such as those of the form

$$\frac{L(\theta_2|X)}{L(\theta_1|X)} = \frac{\alpha P(X|\theta_2)}{\alpha P(X|\theta_1)} = \frac{P(X|\theta_2)}{P(X|\theta_1)} :$$

that are invariant with respect to the constant of proportionality α.

Score

In statistics, the Score or Score function is the partial derivative, with respect to some parameter θ, of the logarithm (commonly the natural logarithm) of the likelihood function. If the observation is X and its likelihood is L(θ;X), then the Score V can be found through the chain rule:

$$V = \frac{\partial}{\partial \theta} \log L(\theta; X) = \frac{1}{L(\theta; X)} \frac{\partial L(\theta; X)}{\partial \theta}.$$

Note that V is a function of θ and the observation X, so that, in general, it is not a statistic. Note also that V indicates the sensitivity of L(θ;X) (its variation normalized by its value.)

Observed Information

In statistics, the Observed information is the negative of the second derivative (the Hessian matrix) of the `log-likelihood` (the logarithm of the likelihood function). It is a sample-based version of the Fisher information.

Suppose we observe random variables $X_1, \ldots, X_n$, independent and identically distributed with density f(X; θ), where θ is a (possibly unknown) vector. Then the log-likelihood of the parameters θ given the data $X_1, \ldots, X_n$ is

$$\ell(\theta | X_1, \ldots, X_n) = \sum_{i=1}^{n} \log f(X_i | \theta)$$

.

We define the Observed information matrix at θ* as

$$\mathcal{J}(\theta^*) = - \left. \nabla \nabla^\top \ell(\theta) \right|_{\theta = \theta^*}$$

$$= - \left. \begin{pmatrix} \frac{\partial^2}{\partial \theta_1^2} & \frac{\partial^2}{\partial \theta_1 \partial \theta_2} & \cdots & \frac{\partial^2}{\partial \theta_1 \partial \theta_n} \\ \frac{\partial^2}{\partial \theta_2 \partial \theta_1} & \frac{\partial^2}{\partial \theta_2^2} & \cdots & \frac{\partial^2}{\partial \theta_2 \partial \theta_n} \\ \vdots & \vdots & \ddots & \vdots \\ \frac{\partial^2}{\partial \theta_n \partial \theta_1} & \frac{\partial^2}{\partial \theta_n \partial \theta_2} & \cdots & \frac{\partial^2}{\partial \theta_n^2} \end{pmatrix} \ell(\theta) \right|_{\theta = \theta^*}$$

Radial basis function	A Radial basis function is a real-valued function whose value depends only on the distance from the origin, so that $\phi(\mathbf{x}) = \phi(\|\mathbf{x}\|)$ or alternatively on the distance from some other point c, called a center, so that $\phi(\mathbf{x}, \mathbf{c}) = \phi(\|\mathbf{x} - \mathbf{c}\|)$. Any function φ that satisfies the property $\phi(\mathbf{x}) = \phi(\|\mathbf{x}\|)$ is a radial function. The norm is usually Euclidean distance, although other distance functions are also possible.
Gradient boosting	Gradient boosting is a machine learning technique for regression problems, which produces a prediction model in the form of an ensemble of weak prediction models, typically decision trees. It builds the model in a stage-wise fashion like other boosting methods do, and it generalizes them by allowing optimization of an arbitrary differentiable loss function. Gradient boosting method can be also used for classification problems, given an appropriate choice of the loss function.
Gibbs sampling	In mathematics and physics, Gibbs sampling is an algorithm to generate a sequence of samples from the joint probability distribution of two or more random variables. The purpose of such a sequence is to approximate the joint distribution, or to compute an integral (such as an expected value). Gibbs sampling is a special case of the Metropolis-Hastings algorithm, and thus an example of a Markov chain Monte Carlo algorithm.

Gibbs sampling is applicable when the joint distribution is not known explicitly, but the conditional distribution of each variable is known. The Gibbs sampling algorithm generates an instance from the distribution of each variable in turn, conditional on the current values of the other variables. It can be shown that the sequence of samples constitutes a Markov chain, and the stationary distribution of that Markov chain is just the sought-after joint distribution.

Markov chain	A Markov chain is a random process with the property that the next state depends only on the current state. It is a Markov model for a particular type of Markov process in which the process can only be in a finite or countable number of states. Markov chains are useful as tools for statistical modeling in almost all fields of modern applied mathematics.
Markov chain Monte Carlo	Markov chain Monte Carlo methods are a class of algorithms for sampling from probability distributions based on constructing a Markov chain that has the desired distribution as its equilibrium distribution. The state of the chain after a large number of steps is then used as a sample from the desired distribution. The quality of the sample improves as a function of the number of steps.
Monte Carlo methods	Monte Carlo methods are a class of computational algorithms that rely on repeated random sampling to compute their results. Monte Carlo methods are often used in simulating physical and mathematical systems. Because of their reliance on repeated computation of random or pseudo-random numbers, these methods are most suited to calculation by a computer and tend to be used when it is unfeasible or impossible to compute an exact result with a deterministic algorithm.
Mean	In statistics, mean has two related meanings: · the arithmetic mean . · the expected value of a random variable, which is also called the population mean. It is sometimes stated that the `mean` means average. This is incorrect if `mean` is taken in the specific sense of `arithmetic mean` as there are different types of averages: the mean, median, and mode.
Mean square error	In statistics, the Mean square error of an estimator is one of many ways to quantify the difference between an estimator and the true value of the quantity being estimated. Mean square error is a risk function, corresponding to the expected value of the squared error loss or quadratic loss. Mean square error measures the average of the square of the `error.` The error is the amount by which the estimator differs from the quantity to be estimated.

Lagrange multiplier	In mathematical optimization, the method of Lagrange multipliers provides a strategy for finding the maximum/minimum of a function subject to constraints.

For example , consider the optimization problem

maximize $f(x, y)$

subject to $g(x, y) = c.$

We introduce a new variable (λ) called a Lagrange multiplier, and study the Lagrange function defined by

$$\Lambda(x, y, \lambda) = f(x, y) + \lambda \cdot \Big(g(x, y) - c \Big).$$

(λ may be either added or subtracted). If (x,y)‰ is a maximum for the original constrained problem, then there exists a λ such that (x,y,λ)‰ is a stationary point for the Lagrange function (stationary points are those points where the partial derivatives of Λ are zero).

Chapter 8. Additive Models, Trees, and Related Methods

Additive model	In statistics, an Additive model is a nonparametric regression method. It was suggested by Jerome H. Friedman and Werner Stuetzle (1981) and is an essential part of the ACE algorithm. The Additive model uses a one dimensional smoother to build a restricted class of nonparametric regression models. Because of this, it is less affected by the curse of dimensionality than e.g. a p-dimensional smoother. Furthermore, the Additive model is more flexible than a standard linear model, while being more interpretable than a general regression surface at the cost of approximation errors. Problems with Additive model include model selection, overfitting, and multicollinearity.

Given a data set $\{y_i, x_{i1}, \ldots, x_{ip}\}_{i=1}^{n}$ of n statistical units, where $\{x_{i1}, \ldots, x_{ip}\}_{i=1}^{n}$ represent predictors and y_i is the outcome, the Additive model takes the form

$$E[y_i | x_{i1}, \ldots, x_{ip}] = \sum_{j=1}^{p} f_j(x_{ij})$$

or

$$Y = \beta_0 + \sum_{j=1}^{p} f_j(X_j) + \varepsilon$$

Where $E[\varepsilon] = 0$, $Var(\varepsilon) = \sigma^2$ and $E[f_j(X_j)] = 0$. The functions $f_j(x_{ij})$ are unknown smooth functions fit from the data. Fitting the Additive model (i.e. the functions f_j) can be done using the backfitting algorithm proposed by Andreas Buja, Trevor Hastie and Robert Tibshirani (1989).

Generalized additive model	In statistics, the Generalized additive model is a statistical model developed by Trevor Hastie and Rob Tibshirani for blending properties of generalized linear models with additive models.

The model specifies a distribution (such as a normal distribution, or a binomial distribution) and a link function g relating the expected value of the distribution to the predictors, and attempts to fit functions f_i to satisfy: |

$$g(\mathrm{E}(Y)) = \beta_0 + f_1(x_1) + f_2(x_2) + \cdots + f_m(x_m).$$

The functions $f_i(x_i)$ may be fit using parametric or non-parametric means, thus providing the potential for better fits to data than other methods. The method hence is very general - a typical Generalized additive model might use a scatterplot smoothing function such as a locally weighted mean for $f_1(x_1)$, and then use a factor model for $f_2(x_2)$.

Link function

In statistics, the generalized linear model (GLM) is a flexible generalization of ordinary least squares regression. The GLM generalizes linear regression by allowing the linear model to be related to the response variable via a Link function and by allowing the magnitude of the variance of each measurement to be a function of its predicted value.

Generalized linear models were formulated by John Nelder and Robert Wedderburn as a way of unifying various other statistical models, including linear regression, logistic regression and Poisson regression, under one framework.

Logistic regression

In statistics, Logistic regression is used for prediction of the probability of occurrence of an event by fitting data to a logit function logistic curve. It is a generalized linear model used for binomial regression. Like many forms of regression analysis, it makes use of several predictor variables that may be either numerical or categorical.

An explanation of Logistic regression begins with an explanation of the logistic function:

$$f(z) = \frac{e^z}{e^z + 1} = \frac{1}{1 + e^{-z}}$$

Degrees of freedom

In statistics, the number of degrees of freedom is the number of values in the final calculation of a statistic that are free to vary.

Estimates of statistical parameters can be based upon different amounts of information or data. The number of independent pieces of information that go into the estimate of a parameter is called the degrees of freedom.

Parameters

In probability theory, one may describe the distribution of a random variable as belonging to a family of probability distributions, distinguished from each other by the values of a finite number of Parameters. For example, one talks about `a Poisson distribution with mean value λ`. The function defining the distribution (the probability mass function) is:

$$f(k; \lambda) = \frac{e^{-\lambda}\lambda^k}{k!}.$$

This example nicely illustrates the distinction between constants, Parameters, and variables e is Euler`s Number, a fundamental mathematical constant.

Decision tree

A Decision tree is a decision support tool that uses a tree-like graph or model of decisions and their possible consequences, including chance event outcomes, resource costs, and utility. Decision trees are commonly used in operations research, specifically in decision analysis, to help identify a strategy most likely to reach a goal. Another use of Decision trees is as a descriptive means for calculating conditional probabilities.

Discrete probability distributions

Discrete probability distributions arise in the mathematical description of probabilistic and statistical problems in which the values that might be observed are restricted to being within a pre-defined list of possible values. This list has either a finite number of members, or at most is countable.

In probability theory, a probability distribution is called discrete if it is characterized by a probability mass function. Thus, the distribution of a random variable X is discrete, and X is then called a discrete random variable, if

$$\sum_u \Pr(X = u) = 1$$

as u runs through the set of all possible values of X.

Linear combination

In mathematics, Linear combinations is a concept central to linear algebra and related fields of mathematics

Chapter 8. Additive Models, Trees, and Related Methods

Suppose that K is a field and V is a vector space over K. As usual, we call elements of V vectors and call elements of K scalars. If $v_1,..v_n$ are vectors and $a_1,..a_n$ are scalars, then the Linear combination of those vectors with those scalars as coefficients is

$$a_1 v_1 + a_2 v_2 + a_3 v_3 + \cdots + a_n v_n$$

In a given situation, K and V may be specified explicitly, or they may be obvious from context. In that case, we often speak of a Linear combination of the vectors $v_1,..v_n$, with the coefficients unspecified (except that they must belong to K). Or, if S is a subset of V, we may speak of a Linear combination of vectors in S, where both the coefficients and the vectors are unspecified, except that the vectors must belong to the set S (and the coefficients must belong to K). Finally, we may speak simply of a Linear combination, where nothing is specified (except that the vectors must belong to V and the coefficients must belong to K).

Specificity

The specificity is a statistical measure of how well a binary classification test correctly identifies the negative cases, or those cases that do not meet the condition under study. That is, the specificity is the proportion of true negatives of all negative cases in the population. It is a parameter of the test.

Rayleigh quotient

In mathematics, for a given complex Hermitian matrix A and nonzero vector x, the Rayleigh quotient R(A,x), is defined as :

$$\frac{x^* A x}{x^* x}.$$

For real matrices and vectors, the condition of being Hermitian reduces to that of being symmetric, and the conjugate transpose x^* to the usual transpose $x`$. Note that R(A,cx) = R(A,x) for any real scalar c. Recall that a Hermitian (or real symmetric) matrix has real eigenvalues.

Inductive reasoning

Inductive reasoning is a kind of reasoning that allows for the possibility that the conclusion is false even where all of the premises are true. The premises of an inductive logical argument indicate some degree of support for the conclusion but do not entail it; i.e. they do not ensure its truth. Induction is employed, for example, in the following argument:

All of the ice we have examined so far is cold.

Therefore, all ice is cold

Multivariate
adaptive regression
splines

Multivariate adaptive regression splines is a form of regression analysis introduced by Jerome Friedman in 1991. It is a non-parametric regression technique and can be seen as an extension of linear models that automatically models non-linearities and interactions.

The term is trademarked and licensed to Salford Systems.

This section introduces Multivariate adaptive regression splines using a few examples. We start with a set of data: a matrix of input variables x, and a vector of the observed responses y, with a response for each row in x. For example, the data could be:

x	y
10.5	16.4
10.7	18.8
10.8	19.7
...	...
20.6	77.0

Here there is only one independent variable, so the x matrix is just a single column. Given these measurements, we would like to build a model which predicts the expected y for a given x.

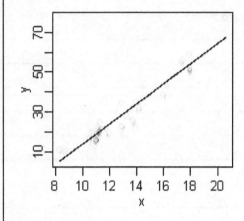

A linear model

A linear model for the above data is

$$\hat{y} = -37 + 5.1x$$

The hat on the $\hat{y}$ indicates that $\hat{y}$ is estimated from the data. The figure on the right shows a plot of this function: a line giving the predicted $\hat{y}$ versus x, with the original values of y shown as red dots.

Chapter 9. Boosting and Additive Trees

Forward selection	In stepwise regression Forward selection involves starting with no variables in the model, trying out the variables one by one and including them if they are `statistically significant`. Usually, this takes the form of a sequence of F-tests, but other techniques are possible, such as t-tests, adjusted R-square, Akaike information criterion, Bayesian information criterion, Mallows` Cp, or false discovery rate.
Loss function	In statistics, decision theory and economics, a Loss function is a function that maps an event onto a real number representing the economic cost or regret associated with the event.
	More specifically, in statistics a Loss function represents the loss (cost in money or loss in utility in some other sense) associated with an estimate being `wrong` (different from either a desired or a true value) as a function of a measure of the degree of wrongness (generally the difference between the estimated value and the true or desired value).
	Given a random variable X over the probability space $(\mathcal{X}, \Sigma, P_\theta)$ determined by a parameter $\theta \in \Theta$, and a set A of possible actions, a decision rule is a function $\delta : \mathcal{X} \to A$.
	A Loss function is a real lower-bounded function L on $\Theta \times A$. The value $L(\theta, \delta)$ is the cost of action $\delta(X)$ under parameter θ.
Gradient boosting	Gradient boosting is a machine learning technique for regression problems, which produces a prediction model in the form of an ensemble of weak prediction models, typically decision trees. It builds the model in a stage-wise fashion like other boosting methods do, and it generalizes them by allowing optimization of an arbitrary differentiable loss function. Gradient boosting method can be also used for classification problems, given an appropriate choice of the loss function.
Overfitting	In statistics, Overfitting occurs when a statistical model describes random error or noise instead of the underlying relationship. Overfitting generally occurs when a model is excessively complex, such as having too many degrees of freedom, in relation to the amount of data available. A model which has been overfit will generally have poor predictive performance, as it can exaggerate minor fluctuations in the data.

Chapter 10. Neural Networks

Projection pursuit	Projection pursuit is a type of statistical technique which involves finding the most `interesting` possible projections in multidimensional data. Often, projections which deviate more from a Normal distribution are considered to be more interesting. As each projection is found, the data are reduced by removing the component along that projection, and the process is repeated to find new projections; this is the `pursuit` aspect that motivated the technique known as matching pursuit.
Radial basis function	A Radial basis function is a real-valued function whose value depends only on the distance from the origin, so that $\phi(\mathbf{x}) = \phi(\|\mathbf{x}\|)$ or alternatively on the distance from some other point c, called a center, so that $\phi(\mathbf{x}, \mathbf{c}) = \phi(\|\mathbf{x} - \mathbf{c}\|)$. Any function φ that satisfies the property $\phi(\mathbf{x}) = \phi(\|\mathbf{x}\|)$ is a radial function. The norm is usually Euclidean distance, although other distance functions are also possible.
Logistic function	A Logistic function or logistic curve is a common sigmoid curve, given its name in 1844 or 1845 by Pierre François Verhulst who studied it in relation to population growth. It can model the `S-shaped` curve of growth of some population P. The initial stage of growth is approximately exponential; then, as saturation begins, the growth slows, and at maturity, growth stops.
	A simple Logistic function may be defined by the formula
	$$P(t) = \frac{1}{1 + e^{-t}}$$
	where the variable P might be considered to denote a population and the variable t might be thought of as time.
Delta rule	The Delta rule is a gradient descent learning rule for updating the weights of the artificial neurons in a single-layer perceptron. It is a special case of the more general backpropagation algorithm. For a neuron j with activation function $g(x)$ the Delta rule for j's i th weight w_{ji} is given by
	$$\Delta w_{ji} = \alpha(t_j - y_j)g'(h_j)x_i$$

where α is a small constant called learning rate, $g(x)$ is the neuron's activation function, t_j is the target output, h_j is the weighted sum of the neuron's inputs, y_j is the actual output, and x_i is the i th input.

Stochastic approximation

Stochastic approximation methods are a family of iterative stochastic optimization algorithms that attempt to find zeroes or extrema of functions which cannot be computed directly, but only estimated via noisy observations. The first, and prototypical, algorithms of this kind were the Robbins-Monro and Kiefer-Wolfowitz algorithms.

In the Robbins-Monro algorithm, introduced in 1951, one has a function M(x) for which one wishes to find the value of x, x_0, satisfying M(x_0) = α. However, what is observable is not M(x), but rather a random variable N(x) such that E = M(x). The algorithm is then to construct a sequence $x_1, x_2, \cdots$ which satisfies

x$_{n+1}$ = x$_n$ + a$_n$(α – N).

Here, $a_1, a_2, \cdots$ is a sequence of positive step sizes. Robbins and Monro proved that, if N(x) is uniformly bounded, M(x) is nondecreasing, M`($x_0$) exists and is positive, and if a$_n$ satisfies a set of bounds (fulfilled if one takes a$_n$ = 1 / n), then x$_n$ converges in L$^2$ to $x_0$.' [Theorem 2]. In general, the a$_n$`s need not equal 1 / n. However, to ensure convergence, they should converge to zero, and in order to average out the noise in N(x), they should converge slowly.

In the Kiefer-Wolfowitz algorithm, introduced a year after the Robbins-Monro algorithm, one wishes to find the maximum, x_0, of the unknown M(x) and constructs a sequence $x_1, x_2, \cdots$ such that

$$x_{n+1} = x_n + a_n \frac{N(x_n + c_n) - N(x_n - c_n)}{c_n}.$$

Early stopping

In machine learning, Early stopping is a form of regularization used when a machine learning model (such as a neural network) is trained by on-line gradient descent. In Early stopping, the training set is split into a new training set and a validation set. Gradient descent is applied to the new training set.

Chapter 10. Neural Networks

Scaling	In the social sciences, scaling is the process of measuring or ordering entities with respect to quantitative attributes or traits. For example, a scaling technique might involve estimating individuals` levels of extraversion, or the perceived quality of products. Certain methods of scaling permit estimation of magnitudes on a continuum, while other methods provide only for relative ordering of the entities.
Multilayer perceptron	A Multilayer perceptron is a feedforward artificial neural network model that maps sets of input data onto a set of appropriate output. It is a modification of the standard linear perceptron in that it uses three or more layers of neurons (nodes) with nonlinear activation functions, and is more powerful than the perceptron in that it can distinguish data that is not linearly separable.
	If a Multilayer perceptron has a linear activation function in all neurons, that is, a simple on-off mechanism to determine whether or not a neuron fires, then it is easily proved with linear algebra that any number of layers can be reduced to the standard two-layer input-output model .
Random forest	Random forest is a machine learning ensemble classifier that consists of many decision trees and outputs the class that is the mode of the class`s output by individual trees. The algorithm for inducing a Random forest was developed by Leo Breiman and Adele Cutler, and ` Random forest s` is their trademark. The term came from random decision forests that was first proposed by Tin Kam Ho of Bell Labs in 1995.

105

Chapter 11. Support Vector Machines and Flexible Discriminants/Prototype Methods

Kernel	A Kernel is a weighting function used in non-parametric estimation techniques. Kernels are used in Kernel density estimation to estimate random variables' density functions, or in Kernel regression to estimate the conditional expectation of a random variable. Kernels are also used in time-series, in the use of the periodogram to estimate the spectral density. A Kernel is a non-negative real-valued integrable function K satisfying the following two requirements: $$\int_{-\infty}^{+\infty} K(u)\,du = 1\,;$$ $$K(-u) = K(u) \text{ for all values of } u\,.$$ The first requirement ensures that the method of Kernel density estimation results in a probability density function. The second requirement ensures that the average of the corresponding distribution is equal to that of the sample used.
Support vector machines	Support vector machines are a set of related supervised learning methods used for classification and regression. Viewing input data as two sets of vectors in an n-dimensional space, an Support vector machines will construct a separating hyperplane in that space, one which maximizes the margin between the two data sets. To calculate the margin, two parallel hyperplanes are constructed, one on each side of the separating hyperplane, which are 'pushed up against' the two data sets.
Hilbert space	The mathematical concept of a Hilbert space generalizes the notion of Euclidean space. It extends the methods of vector algebra and calculus from the two-dimensional Euclidean plane and three-dimensional space to spaces with any finite or infinite number of dimensions. A Hilbert space is an abstract vector space possessing the structure of an inner product that allows length and angle to be measured.
Reproducing kernel Hilbert space	In functional analysis (a branch of mathematics), a Reproducing kernel Hilbert space is a Hilbert space of functions in which pointwise evaluation is a continuous linear functional. Equivalently, they are spaces that can be defined by reproducing kernels. The subject was originally and simultaneously developed by Nachman Aronszajn (1907-1980) and Stefan Bergman (1895-1977) in 1950. An important subset of the Reproducing kernel Hilbert spaces are the Reproducing kernel Hilbert spaces associated to a continuous kernel. These spaces have wide applications, including complex analysis, quantum mechanics and harmonic analysis.

Let X be an arbitrary set and H a Hilbert space of complex-valued functions on X. We say that H is a Reproducing kernel Hilbert space if every linear map of the form

$$L_x : f \mapsto f(x)$$

from H to the complex numbers is continuous for any x in X. By the Riesz representation theorem, this implies that for every x in X there exists a unique element K_x of H with the property that:

$$f(x) = \langle f,\ K_x \rangle \quad \forall f \in H \quad (*).$$

The function K_x is called the point-evaluation functional at the point x.

Since H is a space of functions, the element K_x is itself a function and can therefore be evaluated at every point. We define the function $K : X \times X \to \mathbb{C}$ by

$$K(x,y) \overset{\text{def}}{=} \overline{K_x(y)}.$$

This function is called the reproducing kernel for the Hilbert space H and it is determined entirely by H because the Riesz representation theorem guarantees, for every x in X, that the element K_x satisfying (*) is unique.

Interaction

Interaction is a kind of action that occurs as two or more objects have an effect upon one another. The idea of a two-way effect is essential in the concept of Interaction, as opposed to a one-way causal effect. A closely related term is interconnectivity, which deals with the Interactions of Interactions within systems: combinations of many simple Interactions can lead to surprising emergent phenomena.

Linear discriminant analysis	Linear discriminant analysis and the related Fisher`s linear discriminant are methods used in statistics, pattern recognition and machine learning to find a linear combination of features which characterize or separate two or more classes of objects or events. The resulting combination may be used as a linear classifier, or, more commonly, for dimensionality reduction before later classification.
	Linear discriminant analysis is closely related to ANOVA (analysis of variance) and regression analysis, which also attempt to express one dependent variable as a linear combination of other features or measurements. In the other two methods however, the dependent variable is a numerical quantity, while for Linear discriminant analysis it is a categorical variable (i.e. the class label). Logistic regression and probit regression are more similar to Linear discriminant analysis, as they also explain a categorical variable. These other methods are preferable in applications where it is not reasonable to assume that the independent variables are normally distributed, which is a fundamental assumption of the Linear discriminant analysis method.
Mahalanobis distance	In statistics, Mahalanobis distance is a distance measure introduced by P. C. Mahalanobis in 1936. It is based on correlations between variables by which different patterns can be identified and analyzed. It is a useful way of determining similarity of an unknown sample set to a known one. It differs from Euclidean distance in that it takes into account the correlations of the data set and is scale-invariant, i.e. not dependent on the scale of measurements.
	Formally, the Mahalanobis distance of a multivariate vector $x = \left(x_1, x_2, x_3, \ldots, x_N\right)^T$ from a group of values with mean $\mu = \left(\mu_1, \mu_2, \mu_3, \ldots, \mu_N\right)^T$ and covariance matrix S is defined as:
	$$D_M(x) = \sqrt{(x - \mu)^T S^{-1} (x - \mu)}.$$
Nonparametric regression	Nonparametric regression is a form of regression analysis in which the predictor does not take a predetermined form but is constructed according to information derived from the data. Nonparametric regression requires larger sample sizes than regression based on parametric models because the data must supply the model structure as well as the model estimates.
	Kernel regression estimates the continuous dependent variable from a limited set of data points by convolving the data points` locations with a kernel function - approximately speaking, the kernel function specifies how to `blur` the influence of the data points so that their values can be used to predict the value for nearby locations.

Variance	In probability theory and statistics, the Variance is used as one of several descriptors of a distribution. It describes how far values lie from the mean. In particular, the Variance is one of the moments of a distribution.
K-means clustering	In statistics and machine learning, k-means clustering is a method of cluster analysis which aims to partition n observations into k clusters in which each observation belongs to the cluster with the nearest mean. It is similar to the expectation-maximization algorithm for mixtures of Gaussians in that they both attempt to find the centers of natural clusters in the data.

Given a set of observations $(x_1, x_2, â€¦, x_n)$, where each observation is a d-dimensional real vector, then k-means clustering aims to partition the n observations into k sets (k < n) $S=\{S_1, S_2, â€¦, S_k\}$ so as to minimize the within-cluster sum of squares (WCSS):

$$\underset{\mathbf{S}}{\arg\min} \sum_{i=1}^{k} \sum_{\mathbf{x}_j \in S_i} \left\| \mathbf{x}_j - \boldsymbol{\mu}_i \right\|^2$$

where μ_i is the mean of points in S_i.

Dimension reduction	In statistics, Dimension reduction is the process of reducing the number of random variables under consideration, and can be divided into feature selection and feature extraction.
	Feature selection approaches try to find a subset of the original variables (also called features or attributes). Two strategies are filter (e.g. information gain) and wrapper (e.g. search guided by the accuracy) approaches.
Sliced inverse regression	Sliced inverse regression is a tool for dimension reduction in the field of multivariate statistics.

In statistics, regression analysis is a popular way of studying the relationship between a response variable y and its explanatory variable $\underline{x}$, which is a p-dimensional vector. There are several approaches which come under the term of regression. We know parametric methods, such as multiple linear regression, but also non-parametric techniques, such as local smoothing. If we have high-dimensional data, the number of observations needed to use local smoothing methods escalates exponentially. Therefore we need a tool for dimension reduction, which reveals us the most important directions of the data, on which it can be projected without losing, in the best case, any information. Sliced inverse regression uses the inverse regression curve, $E\left(\underline{x}\,|\,y\right)$, which falls into the effective dimension reducing space under certain conditions, to perform a weighted principal component analysis, with which one identifies the effective dimension reducing directions.

Market basket	The term Market basket or commodity bundle refers to a fixed list of items used specifically to track the progress of inflation in an economy or specific market.
	The most common type of Market basket is the basket of consumer goods, used to define the Consumer Price Index (CPI). Other types of baskets are used to define
	· Producer Price Index (PPI), previously known as Wholesale Price Index (WPI)
	· various commodity price indices
	The term Market basket analysis in the retail business refers to research that provides the retailer with information to understand the purchase behaviour of a buyer. This information will enable the retailer to understand the buyer's needs and rewrite the store's layout accordingly, develop cross-promotional programs, or even capture new buyers (much like the cross-selling concept).
Monte Carlo methods	Monte Carlo methods are a class of computational algorithms that rely on repeated random sampling to compute their results. Monte Carlo methods are often used in simulating physical and mathematical systems. Because of their reliance on repeated computation of random or pseudo-random numbers, these methods are most suited to calculation by a computer and tend to be used when it is unfeasible or impossible to compute an exact result with a deterministic algorithm.
Inductive reasoning	Inductive reasoning is a kind of reasoning that allows for the possibility that the conclusion is false even where all of the premises are true. The premises of an inductive logical argument indicate some degree of support for the conclusion but do not entail it; i.e. they do not ensure its truth. Induction is employed, for example, in the following argument:
	All of the ice we have examined so far is cold. Therefore, all ice is cold
Mode	In statistics, the Mode is the value that occurs the most frequently in a data set or a probability distribution. In some fields, notably education, sample data are often called scores, and the sample Mode is known as the modal score.

Chapter 12. Unsupervised Learning

Like the statistical mean and the median, the Mode is a way of capturing important information about a random variable or a population in a single quantity.

K-means clustering

In statistics and machine learning, k-means clustering is a method of cluster analysis which aims to partition n observations into k clusters in which each observation belongs to the cluster with the nearest mean. It is similar to the expectation-maximization algorithm for mixtures of Gaussians in that they both attempt to find the centers of natural clusters in the data.

Given a set of observations $(x_1, x_2, â€¦, x_n)$, where each observation is a d-dimensional real vector, then k-means clustering aims to partition the n observations into k sets (k < n) $S=\{S_1, S_2, â€¦, S_k\}$ so as to minimize the within-cluster sum of squares (WCSS):

$$\arg\min_{\mathbf{S}} \sum_{i=1}^{k} \sum_{\mathbf{x}_j \in S_i} \|\mathbf{x}_j - \boldsymbol{\mu}_i\|^2$$

where μ_i is the mean of points in S_i.

Lossy compression

In information technology, Lossy compression is a data encoding method which discards (loses) some of the data, in order to achieve its goal, with the result that decompressing the data yields content that is different from the original, though similar enough to be useful in some way. Lossy compression is most commonly used to compress multimedia data (audio, video, still images), especially in applications such as streaming media and internet telephony. By contrast, lossless compression is required for text and data files, such as bank records, text articles, etc.

Hierarchical clustering

In statistics, Hierarchical clustering is a method of cluster analysis which seeks to build a hierarchy of clusters. Strategies for Hierarchical clustering generally fall into two types:

· Agglomerative: This is a `bottom up` approach: each observation starts in its own cluster, and pairs of clusters are merged as one moves up the hierarchy.

· Divisive: This is a `top down` approach: all observations start in one cluster, and splits are performed recursively as one moves down the hierarchy.

In general, the merges and splits are determined in a greedy manner. The results of Hierarchical clustering are usually presented in a dendrogram.

Singular value decomposition

In linear algebra, the Singular value decomposition is an important factorization of a rectangular real or complex matrix, with many applications in signal processing and statistics. Applications which employ the Singular value decomposition include computing the pseudoinverse, least squares fitting of data, matrix approximation, and determining the rank, range and null space of a matrix.

Suppose M is an m×n matrix whose entries come from the field K, which is either the field of real numbers or the field of complex numbers. Then there exists a factorization of the form

$$M = U\Sigma V^*,$$

where U is an m×m unitary matrix over K, the matrix Σ is an m×n diagonal matrix with nonnegative real numbers on the diagonal, and V* denotes the conjugate transpose of V, an n×n unitary matrix over K. Such a factorization is called the singular-value decomposition of M.

Kernel

A Kernel is a weighting function used in non-parametric estimation techniques. Kernels are used in Kernel density estimation to estimate random variables` density functions, or in Kernel regression to estimate the conditional expectation of a random variable. Kernels are also used in time-series, in the use of the periodogram to estimate the spectral density.
A Kernel is a non-negative real-valued integrable function K satisfying the following two requirements:

$$\int_{-\infty}^{+\infty} K(u)\,du = 1\,;$$

$$. K(-u) = K(u) \text{ for all values of } u.$$

The first requirement ensures that the method of Kernel density estimation results in a probability density function. The second requirement ensures that the average of the corresponding distribution is equal to that of the sample used.

| Non-negative matrix factorization | Non-negative matrix factorization is a group of algorithms in multivariate analysis and linear algebra where a matrix, $\mathbf{X}$, is factorized into (usually) two matrices, $\mathbf{W}$ and $\mathbf{H}$: |

$$\text{nmf}(\mathbf{X}) \rightarrow \mathbf{W}\mathbf{H}$$

Factorization of matrices is generally non-unique, and a number of different methods of doing so have been developed by incorporating different constraints; Non-negative matrix factorization differs from these methods in that it enforces the constraint that the factors W and H must be non-negative, i.e., all elements must be equal to or greater than zero.

In chemometrics Non-negative matrix factorization has a long history under the name `self modeling curve resolution`. In this framework the vectors in the right matrix are continuous curves rather than discrete vectors.

| Information theory | Information theory is a branch of applied mathematics and electrical engineering involving the quantification of information. Information theory was developed by Claude E. Shannon to find fundamental limits on signal processing operations such as compressing data and on reliably storing and communicating data. Since its inception it has broadened to find applications in many other areas, including statistical inference, natural language processing, cryptography generally, networks other than communication networks -- as in neurobiology, the evolution and function of molecular codes, model selection in ecology, thermal physics, quantum computing, plagiarism detection and other forms of data analysis. |

| Projection pursuit | Projection pursuit is a type of statistical technique which involves finding the most `interesting` possible projections in multidimensional data. Often, projections which deviate more from a Normal distribution are considered to be more interesting. As each projection is found, the data are reduced by removing the component along that projection, and the process is repeated to find new projections; this is the `pursuit` aspect that motivated the technique known as matching pursuit. |

Chapter 12. Unsupervised Learning

Multidimensional scaling	Multidimensional scaling is a set of related statistical techniques often used in information visualization for exploring similarities or dissimilarities in data. Multidimensional scaling is a special case of ordination. An Multidimensional scaling algorithm starts with a matrix of item-item similarities, then assigns a location to each item in N-dimensional space, where N is specified a priori. For sufficiently small N, the resulting locations may be displayed in a graph or 3D visualisation.
Significance Analysis of Microarrays	Significance analysis of microarrays is a statistical technique, established in 2001 by Tusher, Tibshirani and Chu, for determining whether changes in gene expression are statistically significant. With the advent of DNA microarrays it is now possible to measure the expression of thousands of genes in a single hybridization experiment. The data generated is considerable and a method for sorting out what is significant and what is and is not essential. Significance analysis of microarrays identifies statistically significant genes by carrying out gene specific t-tests and computes a statistic d_j for each gene j, which measures the strength of the relationship between gene expression and a response variable [1,7,8]. This analysis uses non-parametric statistics, since the data may not follow a normal distribution. The response variable describes and groups the data based on experimental conditions. In this method, repeated permutations of the data are used to determine if the expression of any gene is significant related to the response.
PageRank	PageRank is a link analysis algorithm used by the Google Internet search engine that assigns a numerical weighting to each element of a hyperlinked set of documents, such as the World Wide Web, with the purpose of `measuring` its relative importance within the set. The algorithm may be applied to any collection of entities with reciprocal quotations and references. The numerical weight that it assigns to any given element E is referred to as the PageRank of E and denoted by PR(E). The name `PageRank` is a trademark of Google, and the PageRank process has been patented .
Power	The Power of a statistical test is the probability that the test will reject a false null hypothesis (i.e. that it will not make a Type II error). As Power increases, the chances of a Type II error decrease. The probability of a Type II error is referred to as the false negative rate (β). Therefore Power is equal to $1 - \beta$.

Chapter 13. Random Forests/Ensemble Learning

Random forest	Random forest is a machine learning ensemble classifier that consists of many decision trees and outputs the class that is the mode of the class`s output by individual trees. The algorithm for inducing a Random forest was developed by Leo Breiman and Adele Cutler, and ` Random forest s` is their trademark. The term came from random decision forests that was first proposed by Tin Kam Ho of Bell Labs in 1995.
Variance	In probability theory and statistics, the Variance is used as one of several descriptors of a distribution. It describes how far values lie from the mean. In particular, the Variance is one of the moments of a distribution.
Variance reduction	In mathematics, more specifically in the theory of Monte Carlo methods, Variance reduction is a procedure used to increase the precision of the estimates that can be obtained for a given number of iterations. Every output random variable from the simulation is associated with a variance which limits the precision of the simulation results. In order to make a simulation statistically efficient, i.e., to obtain a greater precision and smaller confidence intervals for the output random variable of interest, Variance reduction techniques can be used.
Bias	In statistics, Bias is systematic favoritism that is present in the data collection process resulting in misleading results. There are several types of statistical Bias:
	· Selection Bias, where there is an error in choosing the individuals or groups to take part in a scientific study. It includes sampling Bias, in which some members of the population are more likely to be included than others. Spectrum Bias consists of evaluating the ability of a diagnostic test in a Biased group of patients, which leads to an overestimate of the sensitivity or specificity of the test. Funding Bias may lead to selection of outcomes, test samples, or test procedures that favor a study`s financial sponsor.
	· The Bias of an estimator is the difference between an estimator`s expectation and the true value of the parameter being estimated. Omitted-variable Bias is the Bias that appears in estimates of parameters in a regression analysis when the assumed specification is incorrect, in that it omits an independent variable that should be in the model.
	· In statistical hypothesis testing, a test is said to be unBiased when the probability of rejecting the null hypothesis exceeds the significance level when the alternative is true and is less than or equal to the significance level when the null hypothesis is true.
	· Systematic Bias or systemic Bias are external influences that may affect the accuracy of statistical measurements.

· Data-snooping Bias comes from the misuse of data mining techniques.

Ensemble methods	In statistics and machine learning, ensemble methods use multiple models to obtain better predictive performance than could be obtained from any of the constituent models.
	Unlike a statistical ensemble in statistical mechanics, which is usually infinite, a machine learning ensemble refers only to a concrete finite set of alternative models.
	Supervised learning algorithms are commonly described as performing the task of searching through a hypothesis space to find a suitable hypothesis that will make good predictions with a particular problem.
Forward selection	In stepwise regression Forward selection involves starting with no variables in the model, trying out the variables one by one and including them if they are `statistically significant`. Usually, this takes the form of a sequence of F-tests, but other techniques are possible, such as t-tests, adjusted R-square, Akaike information criterion, Bayesian information criterion, Mallows` Cp, or false discovery rate.
Importance sampling	In statistics, Importance sampling is a general technique for estimating properties of a particular distribution, while only having samples generated from a different distribution rather than the distribution of interest. Depending on the application, the term may refer to the process of sampling from this alternative distribution, the process of inference, or both.
	More formally, let $X : \Omega \to \mathbb{R}$ be a random variable in some probability space $(\Omega, \mathcal{F}, P)$.

Chapter 14. Undirected Graphical Models

Markov property	In probability theory and statistics, the term Markov property refers to a property of a stochastic process. Its namesake is the Russian mathematician Andrey Markov. A stochastic process has the Markov property if the conditional probability distribution of future states of the process depend only upon the present state; that is, given the present, the future does not depend on the past. A process with this property is called a Markov process.
Graphical model	A Graphical model is a probabilistic model for which a graph denotes the conditional independence structure between random variables. They are commonly used in probability theory, statistics--particularly Bayesian statistics--and machine learning. Generally, probabilistic Graphical models use a graph-based representation as the foundation for encoding a complete distribution over a multi-dimensional space and a graph that is a compact or factorized representation of a set of independences that hold in the specific distribution.
Covariance	In probability theory and statistics, covariance is a measure of how much two variables change together. (Variance is a special case of the covariance when the two variables are identical). The covariance between two real-valued random variables X and Y, with expected values $E(X) = \mu$ and $E(Y) = \nu$ is defined as $$\mathrm{Cov}(X, Y) = \mathrm{E}((X - \mu)(Y - \nu)),$$ where E is the expected value operator.
Bayesian Information Criterion	In statistics, the Bayesian information criterion or Schwarz Criterion is a criterion for model selection among a class of parametric models with different numbers of parameters. Choosing a model to optimize Bayesian information criterion is a form of regularization. When estimating model parameters using maximum likelihood estimation, it is possible to increase the likelihood by adding parameters, which may result in overfitting.

Chapter 14. Undirected Graphical Models

Ising model	The Ising model is a mathematical model of ferromagnetism in statistical mechanics. The model consists of discrete variables called spins that can be in one of two states. The spins are arranged in a lattice or graph, and each spin interacts only with its nearest neighbors. The goal is to find phase changes in the Ising model, as a simplified form of phase changes in real substances.
Markov random field	A Markov random field, Markov network or undirected graphical model is a graphical model in which a set of random variables have a Markov property described by an undirected graph. A Markov random field is similar to a Bayesian network in its representation of dependencies. It can represent certain dependencies that a Bayesian network cannot (such as cyclic dependencies); on the other hand, it can`t represent certain dependencies that a Bayesian network can (such as induced dependencies).
Partition function	In statistical mechanics, the partition function Z is an important quantity that encodes the statistical properties of a system in thermodynamic equilibrium. It is a function of temperature and other parameters, such as the volume enclosing a gas. Most of the aggregate thermodynamic variables of the system, such as the total energy, free energy, entropy, and pressure, can be expressed in terms of the partition function or its derivatives.
Gibbs sampling	In mathematics and physics, Gibbs sampling is an algorithm to generate a sequence of samples from the joint probability distribution of two or more random variables. The purpose of such a sequence is to approximate the joint distribution, or to compute an integral (such as an expected value). Gibbs sampling is a special case of the Metropolis-Hastings algorithm, and thus an example of a Markov chain Monte Carlo algorithm. Gibbs sampling is applicable when the joint distribution is not known explicitly, but the conditional distribution of each variable is known. The Gibbs sampling algorithm generates an instance from the distribution of each variable in turn, conditional on the current values of the other variables. It can be shown that the sequence of samples constitutes a Markov chain, and the stationary distribution of that Markov chain is just the sought-after joint distribution.
Markov Chain	A Markov chain is a random process with the property that the next state depends only on the current state. It is a Markov model for a particular type of Markov process in which the process can only be in a finite or countable number of states. Markov chains are useful as tools for statistical modeling in almost all fields of modern applied mathematics.
Markov Chain Monte Carlo	Markov chain Monte Carlo methods are a class of algorithms for sampling from probability distributions based on constructing a Markov chain that has the desired distribution as its equilibrium distribution. The state of the chain after a large number of steps is then used as a sample from the desired distribution. The quality of the sample improves as a function of the number of steps.

Mean	In statistics, mean has two related meanings:
	· the arithmetic mean .
	· the expected value of a random variable, which is also called the population mean. It is sometimes stated that the `mean` means average. This is incorrect if `mean` is taken in the specific sense of `arithmetic mean` as there are different types of averages: the mean, median, and mode.
Minimum description length	The Minimum description length principle is a formalization of Occam`s Razor in which the best hypothesis for a given set of data is the one that leads to the best compression of the data. Minimum description length was introduced by Jorma Rissanen in 1978. It is an important concept in information theory and learning theory.
	Any set of data can be represented by a string of symbols from a finite (say, binary) alphabet.
Monte Carlo methods	Monte Carlo methods are a class of computational algorithms that rely on repeated random sampling to compute their results. Monte Carlo methods are often used in simulating physical and mathematical systems. Because of their reliance on repeated computation of random or pseudo-random numbers, these methods are most suited to calculation by a computer and tend to be used when it is unfeasible or impossible to compute an exact result with a deterministic algorithm.

Chapter 15. High-Dimensional Problems

Linear discriminant analysis	Linear discriminant analysis and the related Fisher`s linear discriminant are methods used in statistics, pattern recognition and machine learning to find a linear combination of features which characterize or separate two or more classes of objects or events. The resulting combination may be used as a linear classifier, or, more commonly, for dimensionality reduction before later classification.
	Linear discriminant analysis is closely related to ANOVA (analysis of variance) and regression analysis, which also attempt to express one dependent variable as a linear combination of other features or measurements. In the other two methods however, the dependent variable is a numerical quantity, while for Linear discriminant analysis it is a categorical variable (i.e. the class label). Logistic regression and probit regression are more similar to Linear discriminant analysis, as they also explain a categorical variable. These other methods are preferable in applications where it is not reasonable to assume that the independent variables are normally distributed, which is a fundamental assumption of the Linear discriminant analysis method.
Kernel	A Kernel is a weighting function used in non-parametric estimation techniques. Kernels are used in Kernel density estimation to estimate random variables` density functions, or in Kernel regression to estimate the conditional expectation of a random variable. Kernels are also used in time-series, in the use of the periodogram to estimate the spectral density. A Kernel is a non-negative real-valued integrable function K satisfying the following two requirements: $$\int_{-\infty}^{+\infty} K(u)\,du = 1\,;$$ $$K(-u) = K(u) \text{ for all values of } u\,.$$ The first requirement ensures that the method of Kernel density estimation results in a probability density function. The second requirement ensures that the average of the corresponding distribution is equal to that of the sample used.
Logistic regression	In statistics, Logistic regression is used for prediction of the probability of occurrence of an event by fitting data to a logit function logistic curve. It is a generalized linear model used for binomial regression. Like many forms of regression analysis, it makes use of several predictor variables that may be either numerical or categorical.

Chapter 15. High-Dimensional Problems

An explanation of Logistic regression begins with an explanation of the logistic function:

$$f(z) = \frac{e^z}{e^z + 1} = \frac{1}{1 + e^{-z}}$$

Dimension reduction

In statistics, Dimension reduction is the process of reducing the number of random variables under consideration, and can be divided into feature selection and feature extraction.

Feature selection approaches try to find a subset of the original variables (also called features or attributes). Two strategies are filter (e.g. information gain) and wrapper (e.g. search guided by the accuracy) approaches.

Singular value decomposition

In linear algebra, the Singular value decomposition is an important factorization of a rectangular real or complex matrix, with many applications in signal processing and statistics. Applications which employ the Singular value decomposition include computing the pseudoinverse, least squares fitting of data, matrix approximation, and determining the rank, range and null space of a matrix.

Suppose M is an m×n matrix whose entries come from the field K, which is either the field of real numbers or the field of complex numbers. Then there exists a factorization of the form

$$M = U\Sigma V^*,$$

where U is an m×m unitary matrix over K, the matrix Σ is an m×n diagonal matrix with nonnegative real numbers on the diagonal, and V* denotes the conjugate transpose of V, an n×n unitary matrix over K. Such a factorization is called the singular-value decomposition of M.

Survival analysis

Survival analysis is a branch of statistics which deals with death in biological organisms and failure in mechanical systems. This topic is called reliability theory or reliability analysis in engineering, and duration analysis or duration modeling in economics or sociology. More generally, Survival analysis involves the modeling of time to event data; in this context, death or failure is considered an `event` in the Survival analysis literature.

Chapter 15. High-Dimensional Problems

Inductive reasoning	Inductive reasoning is a kind of reasoning that allows for the possibility that the conclusion is false even where all of the premises are true. The premises of an inductive logical argument indicate some degree of support for the conclusion but do not entail it; i.e. they do not ensure its truth. Induction is employed, for example, in the following argument: All of the ice we have examined so far is cold. Therefore, all ice is cold
Partial least squares regression	Partial least squares regression is a statistical method that bears some relation to principal components regression; instead of finding hyperplanes of maximum variance between the response and independent variables, it finds a linear regression model by projecting the predicted variables and the observable variables to a new space. Because both the X and Y data are projected to new spaces, the PLS family of methods are known as bilinear factor models. Partial least squares Discriminant Analysis (PLS-DA) It is used to find the fundamental relations between two matrices (X and Y), i.e. a latent variable approach to modeling the covariance structures in these two spaces. A PLS model will try to find the multidimensional direction in the X space that explains the maximum multidimensional variance direction in the Y space. PLS-regression is particularly suited when the matrix of predictors has more variables than observations, and when there is multicollinearity among X values. By contrast, standard regression will fail in these cases. The general underlying model of multivariate PLS is $$X = TP^T + E$$ $$Y = TQ^T + F,$$ where X is an $n \times m$ matrix of predictors, Y is an $n \times p$ matrix of responses, T is an $n \times l$ matrix (the score, component or factor matrix), P and Q are, respectively, $m \times l$ and $p \times l$ loading matrices, and matrices E and F are the error terms, assumed to be i.i.d. normal.
Holm-Bonferroni method	In statistics, the Holm-Bonferroni method performs more than one hypothesis test simultaneously.

Suppose there are k null hypotheses to be tested and the overall type 1 error rate is α. Start by ordering the p-values and comparing the smallest p-value to α/k. If that p-value is less than α/k, then reject that hypothesis and start all over with the same α and test the remaining k – 1 hypothesis, i.e. order the k – 1 remaining p-values and compare the smallest one to α/(k – 1). Continue doing this until the hypothesis with the smallest p-value cannot be rejected. At that point, stop and accept all hypotheses that have not been rejected at previous steps.

False discovery rate	False discovery rate control is a statistical method used in multiple hypothesis testing to correct for multiple comparisons. In a list of rejected hypotheses, False discovery rate controls the expected proportion of incorrectly rejected null hypotheses (type I errors). It is a less conservative procedure for comparison, with greater power than familywise error rate (FWER) control, at a cost of increasing the likelihood of obtaining type I errors.
Significance Analysis of Microarrays	Significance analysis of microarrays is a statistical technique, established in 2001 by Tusher, Tibshirani and Chu, for determining whether changes in gene expression are statistically significant. With the advent of DNA microarrays it is now possible to measure the expression of thousands of genes in a single hybridization experiment. The data generated is considerable and a method for sorting out what is significant and what is and is not essential. Significance analysis of microarrays identifies statistically significant genes by carrying out gene specific t-tests and computes a statistic d_j for each gene j, which measures the strength of the relationship between gene expression and a response variable [1,7,8]. This analysis uses non-parametric statistics, since the data may not follow a normal distribution. The response variable describes and groups the data based on experimental conditions. In this method, repeated permutations of the data are used to determine if the expression of any gene is significant related to the response.
Naive Bayes classifier	A Bayes classifier is a simple probabilistic classifier based on applying Bayes` theorem (from Bayesian statistics) with strong (naive) independence assumptions. A more descriptive term for the underlying probability model would be `independent feature model`.
	In simple terms, a Naive Bayes classifier assumes that the presence (or absence) of a particular feature of a class is unrelated to the presence (or absence) of any other feature.

Printed in August 2021
by Rotomail Italia S.p.A., Vignate (MI) - Italy